WHAT THE FAQ IS BITCOIN?

FAQs & ANSWERS

& scan QR codes for more!

TUNA OZEN
SAADETTIN KONUKSEVEN

WHAT THE FAQ IS BITCOIN ?

EDITOR: Ece Berktav Çelik
COVER DESIGN: Mehmet Mert Budak
3D BITCOIN DESIGN: Serdar Özen
ART DIRECTION: Sezin Aktürk
2019 AUGUST

BY THE AUTHORS OF
"BITCOIN:
AYN RAND
WAS WRONG,
ATLAS
NEVER SHRUGGED!"

faqthebitcoin.com

“I'M BETTER WITH CODE THAN WITH WORDS THOUGH.”

SATOSHI NAKAMOTO

dedicated to

Satoshi Nakamoto

WHEN YOU ACCEPT MONEY IN PAYMENT FOR YOUR EFFORT, YOU DO SO ONLY ON THE CONVICTION THAT YOU WILL EXCHANGE IT FOR THE PRODUCT OF THE EFFORT OF OTHERS. IT IS NOT THE MOOCHERS OR THE LOOTERS WHO GIVE VALUE TO MONEY.

NOT AN OCEAN OF TEARS NOR ALL THE GUNS IN THE WORLD CAN TRANSFORM THOSE PIECES OF PAPER IN YOUR WALLET INTO THE BREAD YOU WILL NEED TO SURVIVE TOMORROW.

THOSE PIECES OF PAPER, WHICH SHOULD HAVE BEEN GOLD, ARE A TOKEN OF HONOR – YOUR CLAIM UPON THE ENERGY OF THE MEN WHO PRODUCE. YOUR WALLET IS YOUR STATEMENT OF HOPE THAT SOMEWHERE IN THE WORLD AROUND YOU THERE ARE MEN WHO WILL NOT DEFAULT ON THAT MORAL PRINCIPLE WHICH IS THE ROOT OF MONEY. IS THIS WHAT YOU CONSIDER EVIL?

AYN RAND / ATLAS SHRUGGED

What you will / will not find in this book?

You will not find financial advice in this book.

You will not find predictions about Bitcoin's price in this book.

You will not find advices for becoming rich overnight in this book.

You will not find a complicated narration that will confuse you with cool buzzwords in this book.

You will find the answers to frequently asked questions about Bitcoin.

FOR A BETTER READING EXPERIENCE AND TO LEARN MORE KEEP CLOSE YOUR MOBILE PHONE WHICH HAS QR CODE READER.

Why does humanity need money?

To Trade!

Trading is what enabled the human race to survive as a species.

Why do we trade?

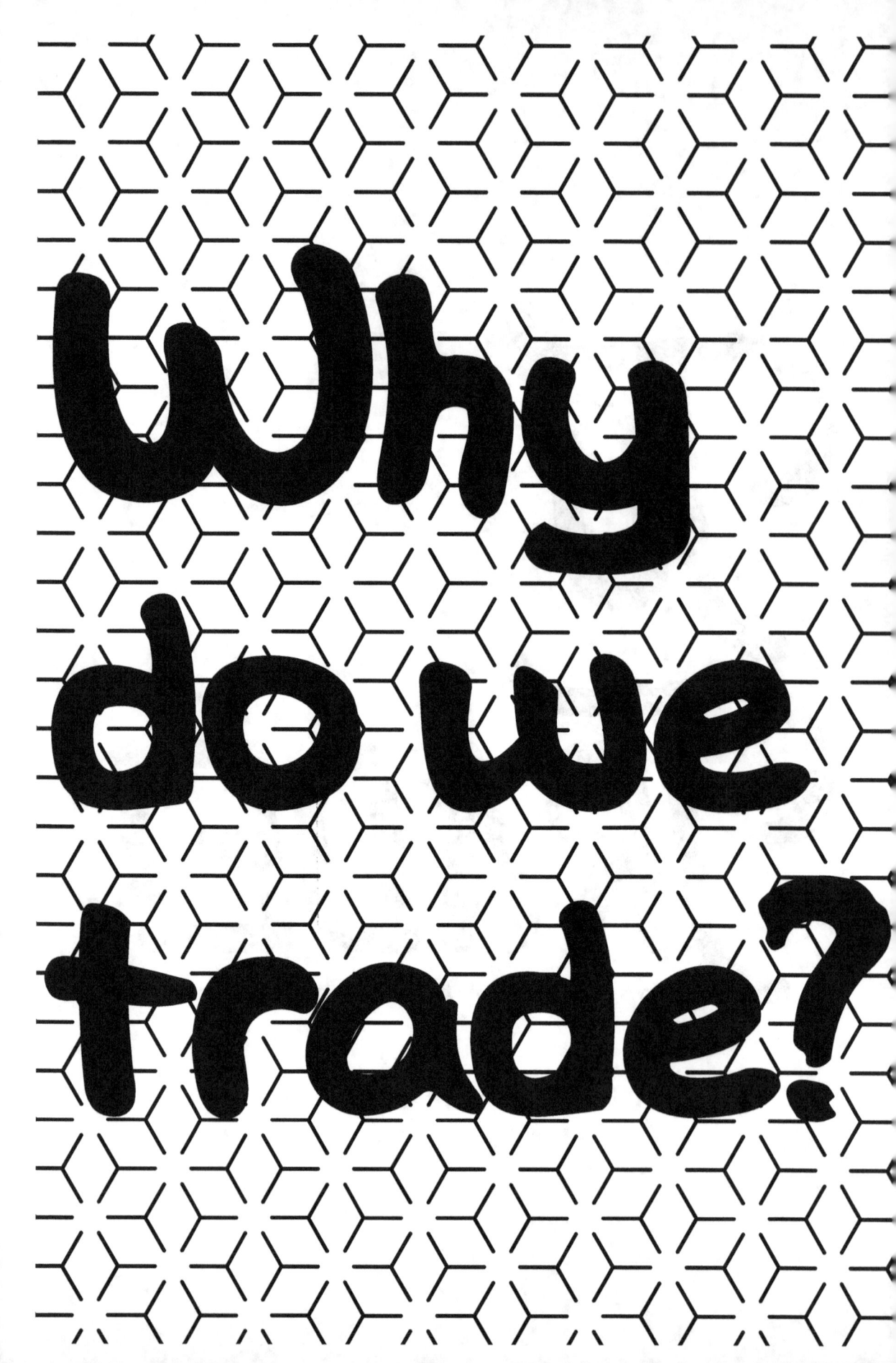

Consider this, can you survive or lead a better life on your own?

Let's say you have sown some wheat, baked your bread, cooked your veggies, built your house, took water from the well..

Can you generate your own electricity?
Can you perform surgery on yourself?

To put it briefly, you need good neighbors.
Trading has allowed humanity
to progress and survive.
Let's take it one step further and say
"trading is what enabled the human race to survive as a species."

From this point of view,
trading is the greatest human invention.

How DID WE START TRADING?

Bartering was the method for trading in the early days of humanity. Bartering allowed people to survive at that time and was sufficient for trading. You could give 1 kg of wheat to cover your need for 2 kg of apples, for instance. But as time passed, bartering became insufficient for humanity's needs. Because it was hard to calculate the exact cross-values of each product. Also, the person with the apples may have needed milk, not wheat. This caused a lack of overlapping between supply and demand. At this point, a common trading tool which meant something for all humans was needed.

Why did we quit bartering?

Besides the "coincidence of wants"

mental cost of transactions is very high in barter economy. Because, you have to know the price of each product against all others for trading to function properly in this economy. For example, you have to know the price of your apples in wheat, barley, coal, etc. This increased the mental cost and made trading harder for humans. We can safely say that the underlying reason for coming up with a common currency was to reduce said mental cost, thereby facilitating trade. Of course, humanity could not achieve a single universal currency. So apples had prices in various currencies in different countries. Yet, the "mental cost" was quite lower compared to bartering.

what are
the most
widespread
currencies used
by mankind,
until bills?

₪ ؋ $ ман лв R$

៛ £

€ ден

1.

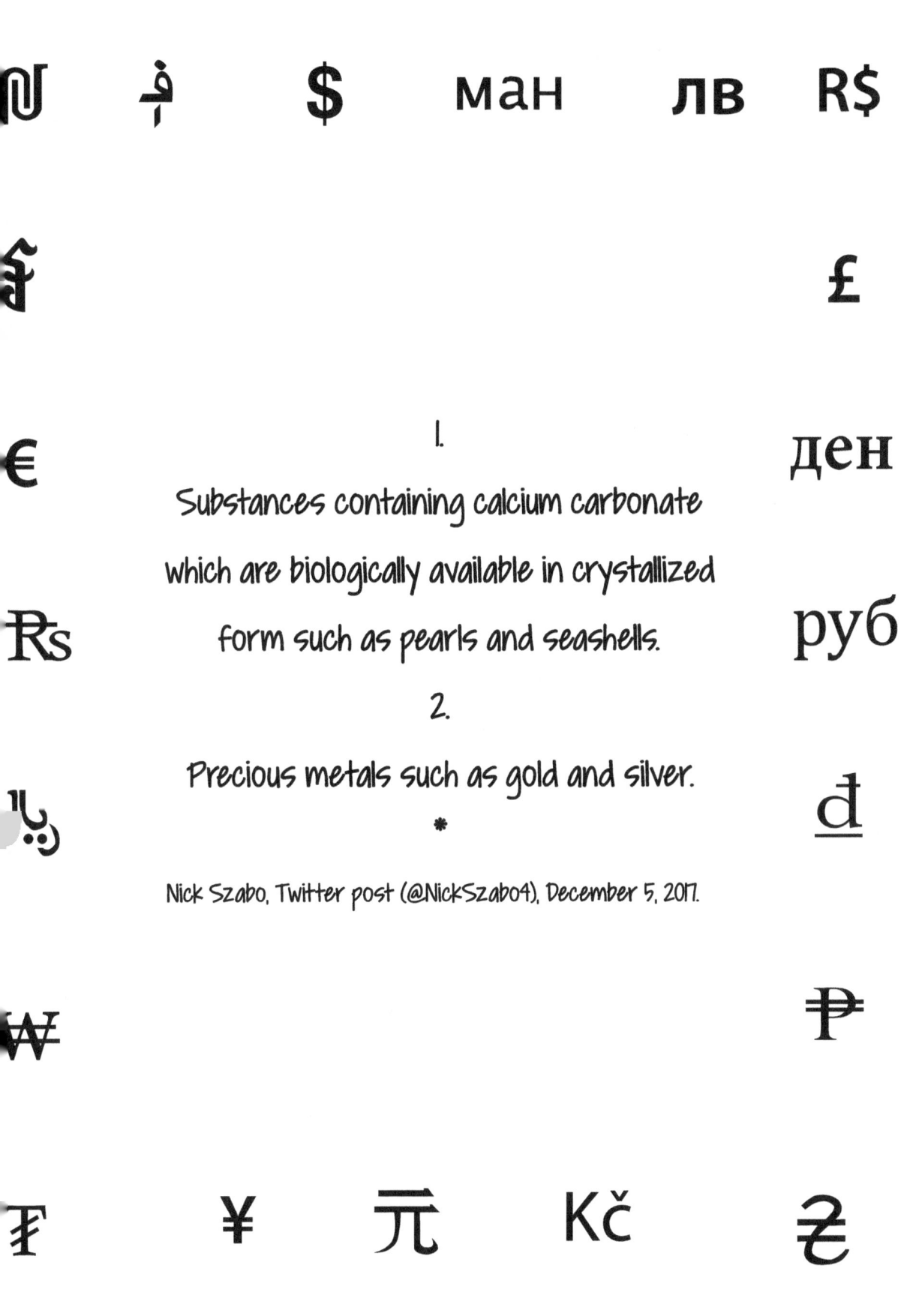

Substances containing calcium carbonate which are biologically available in crystallized form such as pearls and seashells.

₨ руб

2.

Precious metals such as gold and silver.

﷼ ₫

*

Nick Szabo, Twitter post (@NickSzabo4), December 5, 2017.

₩ ₱

₮ ¥ 元 Kč ₴

What is sound money?

Sound money is money that is not prone to sudden appreciation or depreciation in purchasing power over the long term, aided by self-correcting mechanisms inherent in a free-market system.

free-market.*

* To read more about sound money
visit soundmoneydefense.org
or scan the QR code.

Why did humanity choose sound money?

...because humanity has
always tried to protect itself
against inflation
and to have a free trading
tool since day one.

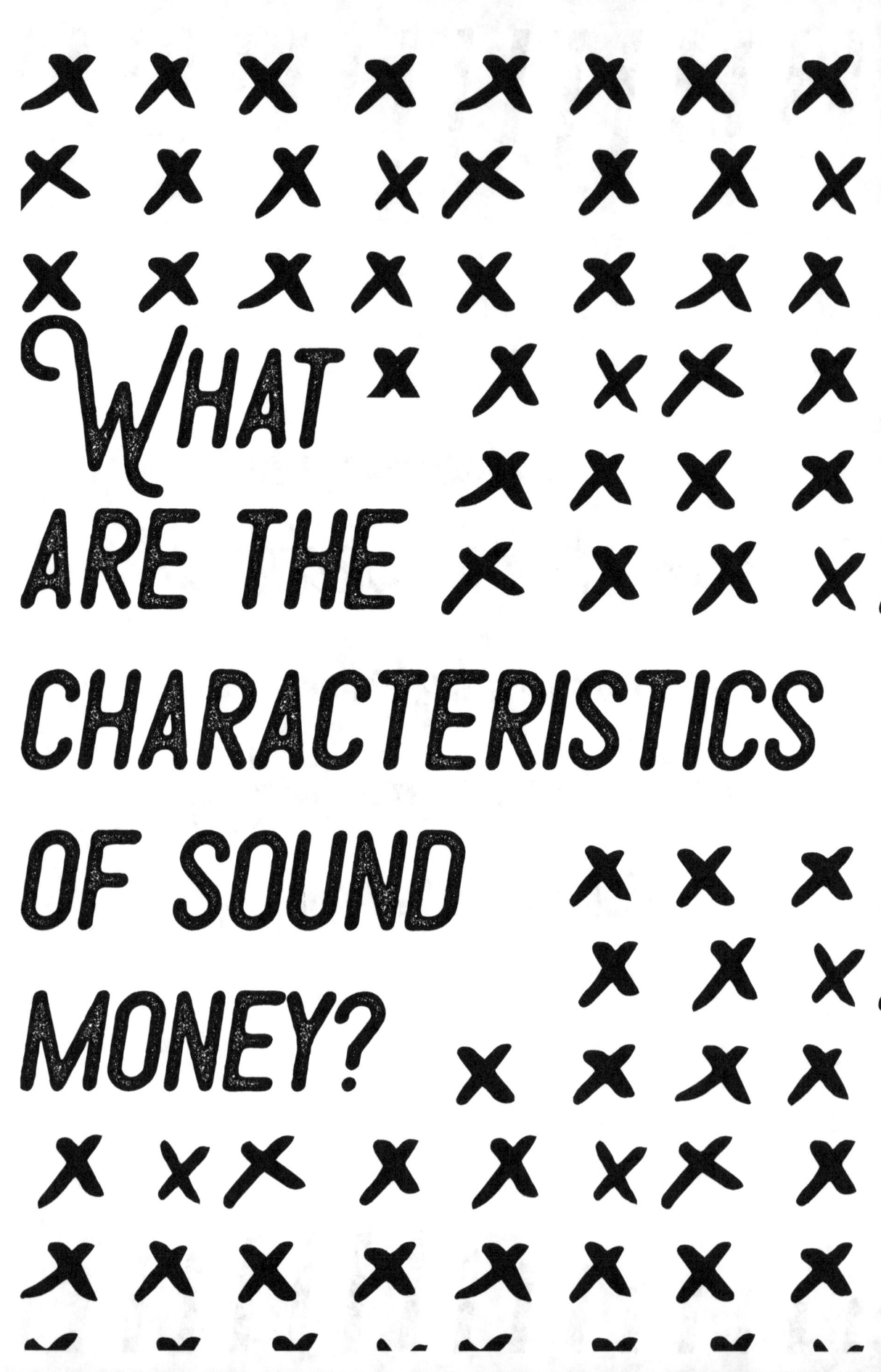

What are the characteristics of sound money?

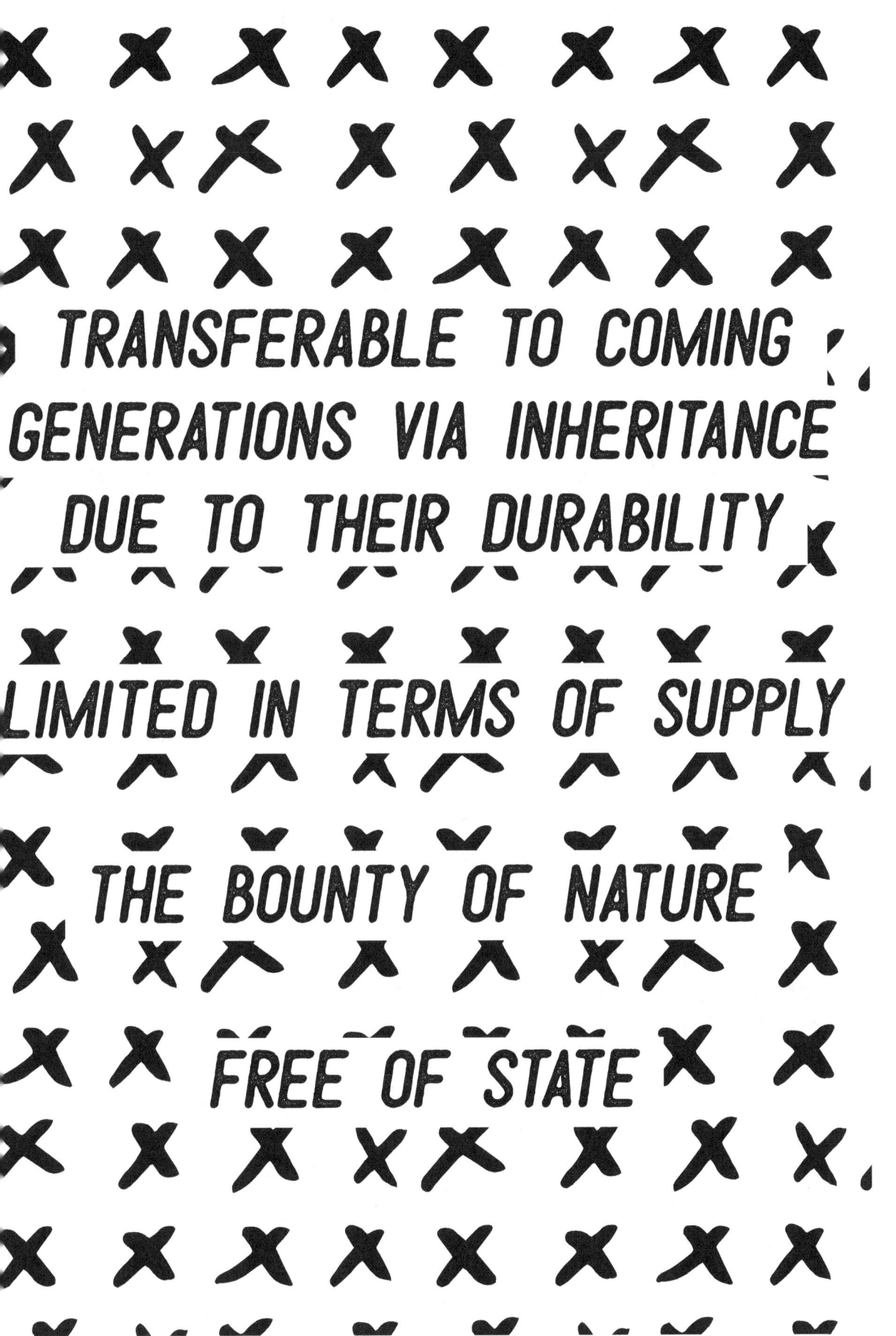

TRANSFERABLE TO COMING GENERATIONS VIA INHERITANCE DUE TO THEIR DURABILITY

LIMITED IN TERMS OF SUPPLY

THE BOUNTY OF NATURE

FREE OF STATE

how was sound money evolved to paper notes?

First, gold backed paper notes.

Then, nothing backed paper notes.

What is the U.S. dollar backed by?

NOTHING!

What is the importance of BRETTON WOODS system?

USA ended the Bretton Woods System on 15 August 1971, when it terminated convertibility of the US dollar to gold. After that date US dollar and other traditional currencies are backed by nothing.
Yes, nothing!

To learn more about
the Bretton Woods system
scan the QRcode.

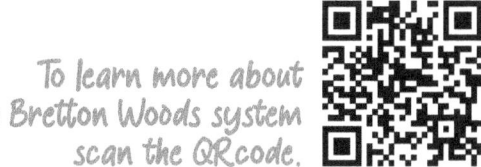

Isn't U.S. dollar backed by gold?

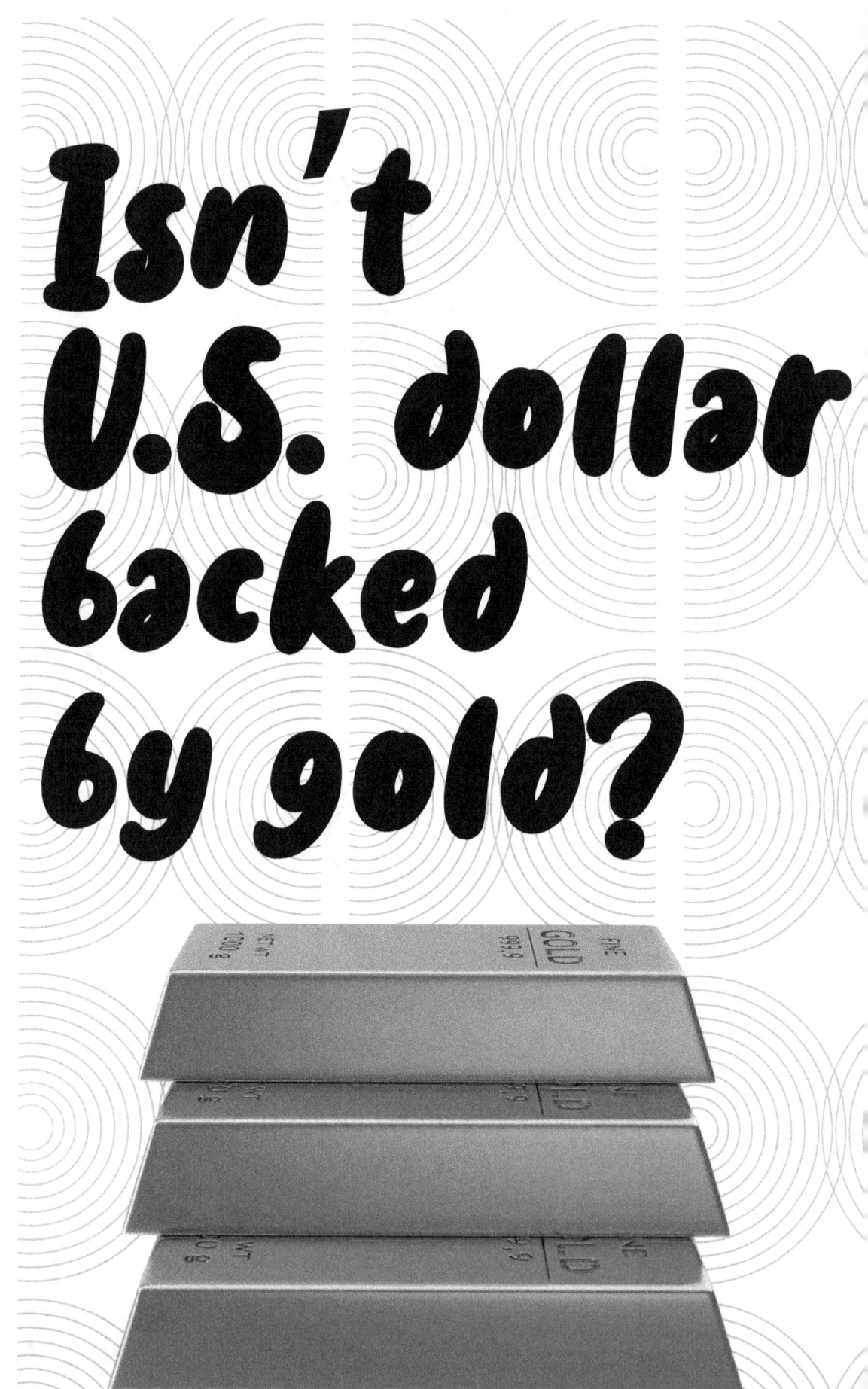

It was backed by gold.

It was UNITED STATES NOTE. NOT FEDERAL RESERVE NOTE

IS THERE A NOTE LIKE THIS ON FEDERAL RESERVE NOTES?

It was backed by silver.

This certified that there had been deposited in the TREASURY of THE UNITED STATES OF AMERICA.

It was payable to the bearer on demand.

Now it is FEDERAL RESERVE NOTE. NOT UNITED STATES NOTE.

Not payable to the bearer on demand?

IN GOD WE TRUST

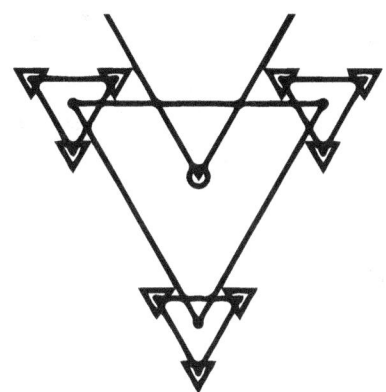

When was this expression added to the dollar?

"In God We Trust" expression was not present on the dollar until 1953. This expression was first added to the dollars printed by the US Treasury in 1953. The bills printed by the Treasury did not have their reserves in "gold or silver" at this given date. They were bills that were printed solely on the basis of trust.

The expression was added to the dollar bills printed by FED from 1965 onwards. This may very well be the biggest change we can observe in money... Transition from a tangible monetary system to a trust-based system...

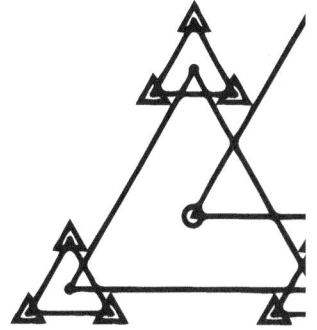

What is it called if a currency is backed by nothing?

Fiat

What is the main problem with fiat currencies?

They're backed
by nothing
other than
full faith and
trust of a
government.

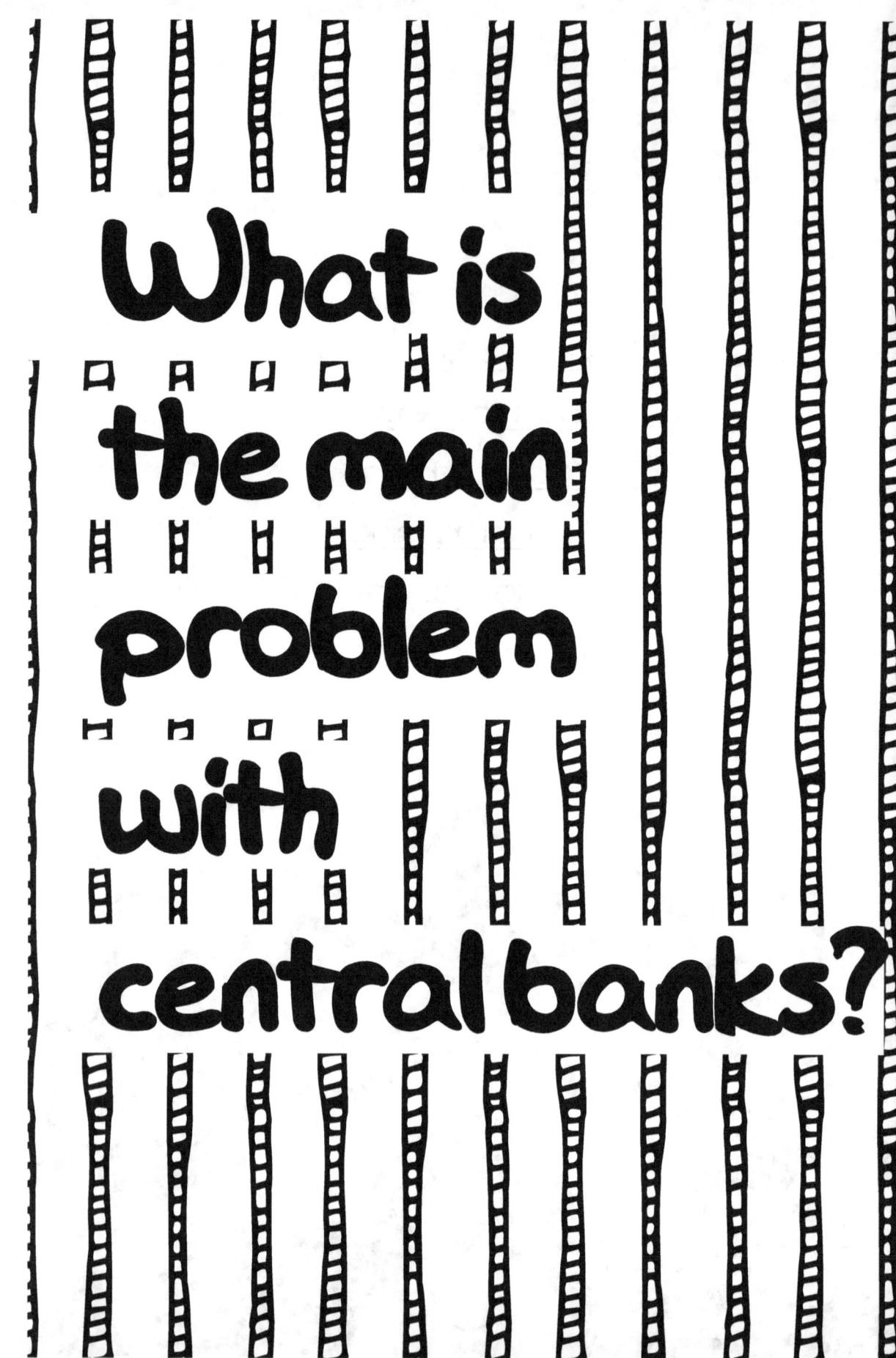

What is the main problem with central banks?

Unlimited Supply

The main problem with central banks is politics. They can change the monetary policy whenever they want. So there is no hard cap for fiat currencies. There is unlimited supply.

So your wealth is can esaily be inflated by central banks.

What is the main problem with the current monetary system?

Current

monetary system is

"Debt Based".

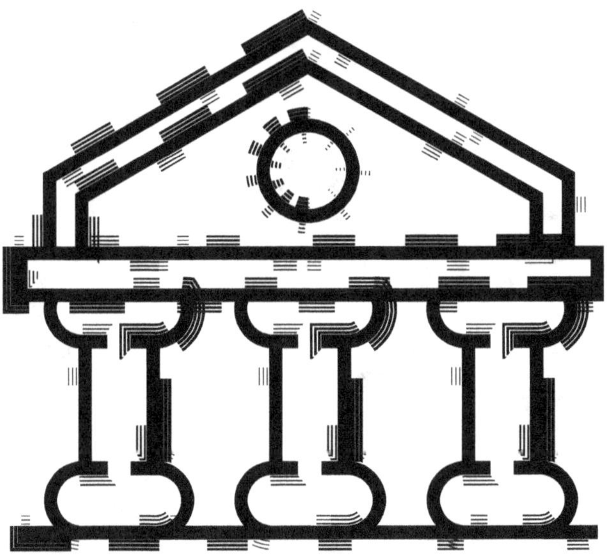

So with "fractional reserve banking" system banks create money out of thin air.

Why the whole banking system is a SCAM?

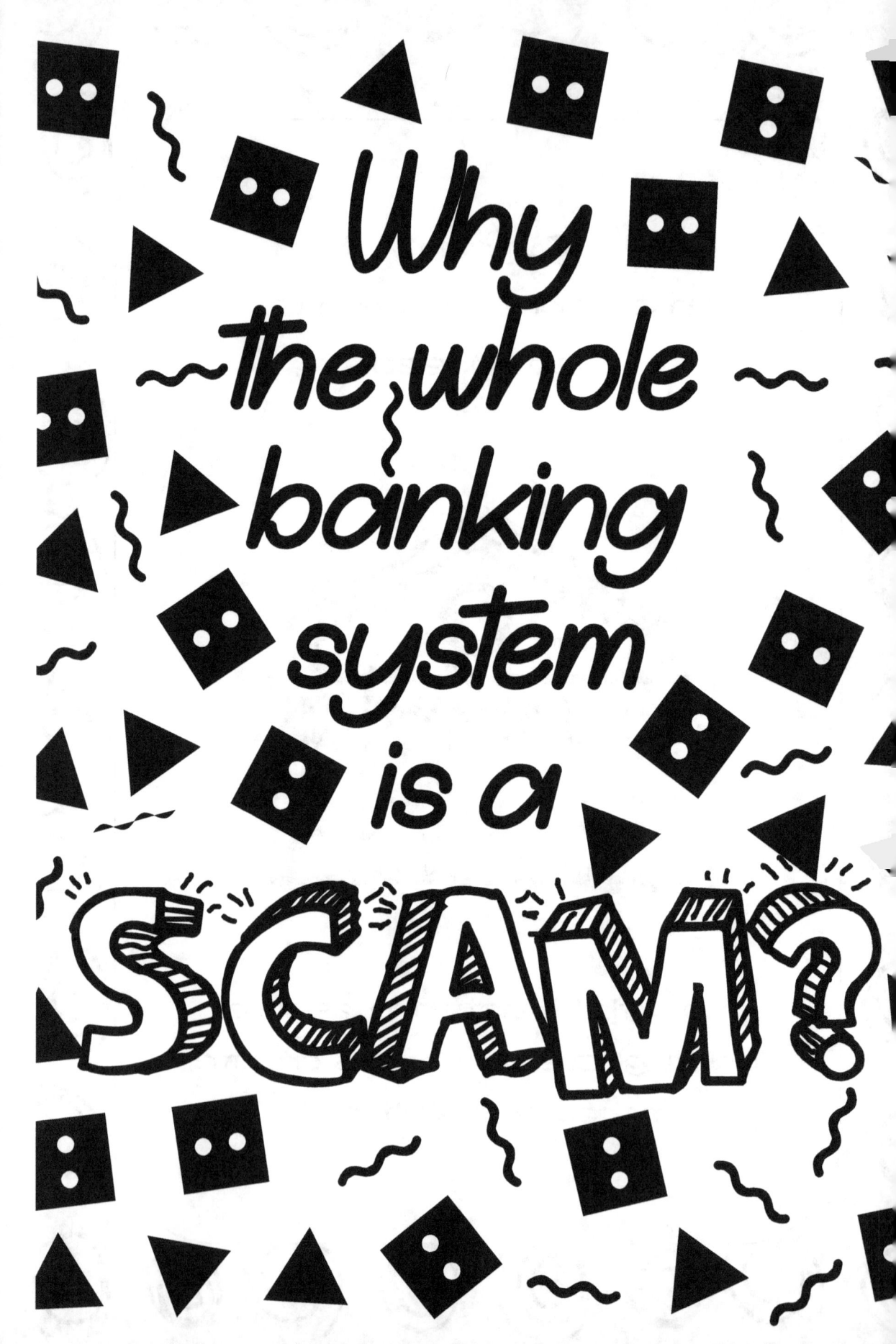

All the banks are broke. Bank of Santander, Deutsche Bank, Royal Bank of Scotland... Why are they broke? It is not an act of God, it is not some sort of tsunami. They are broke because we have a system called "fractional reserve banking".

Which means that banks can lend money that they don't actually have.

It's a criminal scandal and it's been going on for too long.....

Godfrey Bloom
European Parliament, Strasbourg
21 May 2013

To watch the 2 minutes speech of Godfrey Bloom scan the QR code.

BUT

There were always people
who were festered with
the destruction of
gold standard,
who were dreaming of
a banking system and
a currency that are not tied
to any government.

"A FIAT
MONEY SYSTEM
CANNOT GO ON FOREVER
AND MUST ONE DAY
COME TO AN END.
THE QUESTION IS
HOW TO RETURN
TO THEGOLD STANDARD."

LUDWIG VON MOSES

Or "The Bitcoin Standard"?

Scan the QR code to buy "THE BITCOIN STANDARD" book by Saifedean Ammous.

WHY BITCOIN?

Bitcoin was born as a solution for the virtualization of money in the last century, for the loss of guarantee behind money and for the bloated financial system that can no longer be sustained.

who created Bitcoin?

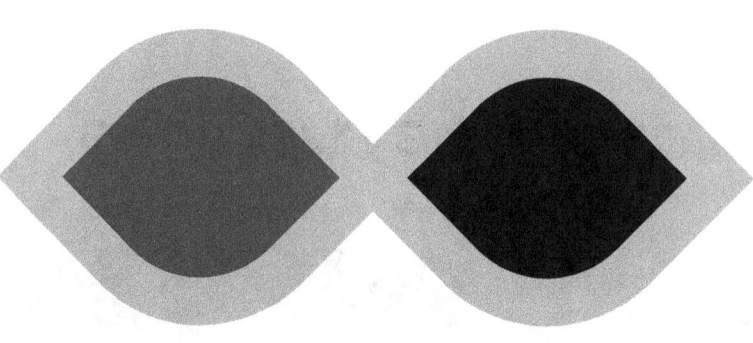

Bitcoin
was invented
by an unknown person
or a group of people
under the pseudonym

SATOSHI NAKAMOTO

Origins of Bitcoin?

"The theoretical roots of Bitcoin can be found in the Austrian school of economics."

European Central Bank

This might be one and only thing upon that we agree with a central bank :)

Search for

Ludwig von Moses

Nation, State, and Economy

Friedrich von Hayek

Denationalisation of Money

Carl Menger

The Origins of Money

Visit mises.org or
scan the QR code to learn more
about Austrian school of economics.

[redacted] WAS [redacted] HAYEK [redacted] DESCRIBING [redacted] BITCOIN [redacted] IN [redacted]

1984?

"I DON'T BELIEVE WE SHALL EVER HAVE A GOOD MONEY AGAIN BEFORE WE TAKE THE THING OUT OF THE HANDS OF GOVERNMENT. **WE CAN'T TAKE IT VIOLENTLY OUT OF THE HANDS OF GOVERNMENT.** ALL CAN DO IS BY SOME SLY ROUNDABOUT WAY INTRODUCE SOMETHING THEY CANNOT STOP."

FRIEDRICH VON HAYEK

1984

CYPHERPUNKS

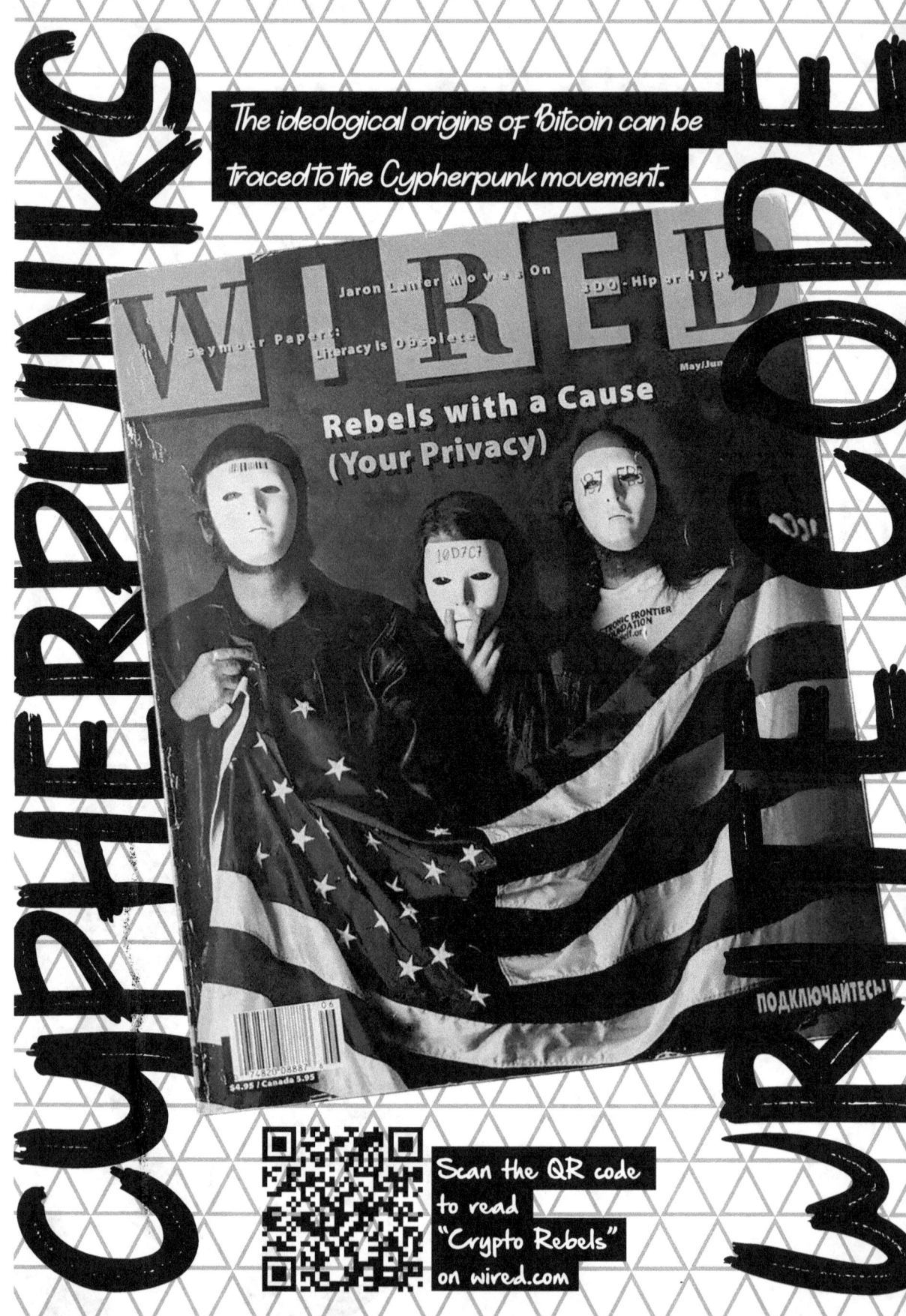

The ideological origins of Bitcoin can be traced to the Cypherpunk movement.

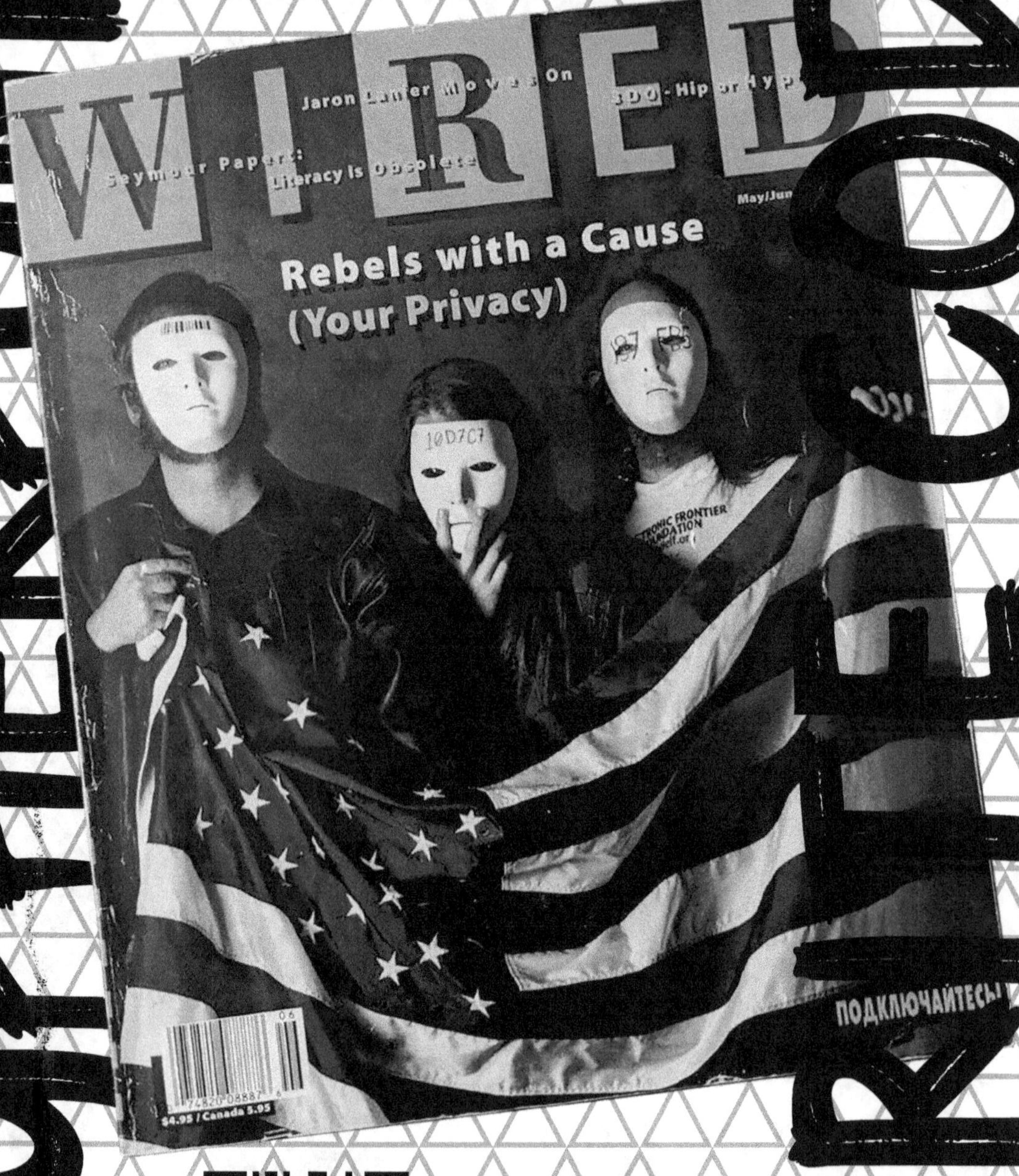

Scan the QR code to read "Crypto Rebels" on wired.com

WIRED CODE

...Therefore, privacy in an open society requires anonymous transaction systems. Until now, cash has been the primary such system. An anonymous transaction system is not a secret transaction system. An anonymous system empowers individuals to reveal their identity when desired and only when desired, this is the essence of privacy...

Eric Hughes
A Cypherpunk's Manifesto"

Scan the QR code to read
"A Cypherpunk's Manifesto" by Eric Hughes.

What does CYPHERPUNKS WRITE CODE mean?

1

"Cypherpunks write code" should be taken metaphorically. I think "to write code" means to take unilateral effective action as an individual. What is important is that Cypherpunks take personal responsibility for empowering themselves against threats to privacy.

TIMOTHY MAY

Scan the QR code to read "The Crypto Anarchist Manifesto" by Timothy May.

"WHO IS JOHN GALT?"

Ayn Rand // Atlas Shrugged

Adam Back
@adam3us

Follow

"Who is Satoshi Nakamoto?" is better left rhetorical, like "Who is John Galt?"

8:43 AM - 11 Dec 2015

"Whenever destroyers appear among men, they start by destroying money, for money is men's protection and the base of a moral existence. Destroyers seize gold and leave to its owners a counterfeit pile of paper. This kills all objective standards and delivers men into the arbitrary power of an arbitrary setter of values. Gold was an objective value, an equivalent of wealth produced.

Paper is a mortgage on wealth that does not exist, backed by a gun aimed at those who are expected to produce it. Paper is a check drawn by legal looters upon an account which is not theirs, upon the virtue of the victims. Watch for the day when it becomes marked.

"Account overdrawn"

AYN RAND // ATLAS SHRUGGED

WHAT ARE THE PRECURSORS TO BITCOIN?

Bitgold

by Nick Szabo

B-money

by Wei Dai

RPOW

by Hal Finney

WHAT IS BIT GOLD?

Satoshi Nakamoto wrote on bitcointalk.org that
Bitcoin was an implementation of b-money and Bitgold.

Scan the QR code to see Satoshi Nakamoto's post.

The closest proposal to Bitcoin came from Nick Szabo in 1997. According to Szabo, precious metals were far more valuable and safe compared to the currencies provided by states. But there were two problems pertaining to precious metals. First, it was nearly impossible to use precious metals in smaller transactions. Second, it was costly and problematic to handle precious metals from one place to another due to issues such as safety and accidents.

Scan the QR code to see Nick Szabo's Bitgold proposal.

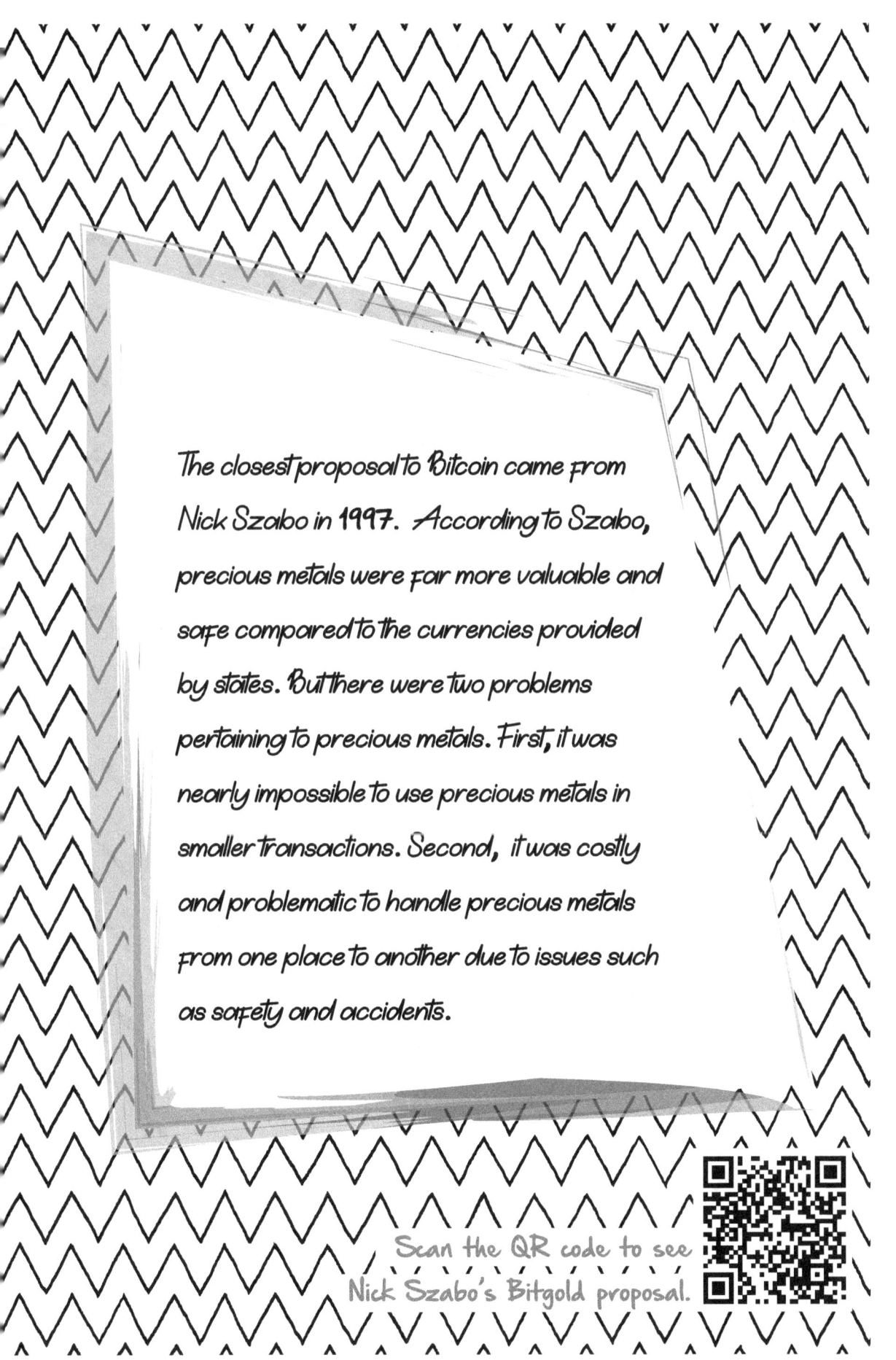

How did Nick Szabo come with BitGold?

Nick Szabo
@NickSzabo4

@NickSzabo4 @AStulkowski ve diğer 3 kişiye yanıt olarak

More specifically: from computer security protocols I got the principle of trust minimization, from that principle & studying how gold IOUs ultimately failed, figuring out how to implement the properties of gold in cyberspace.

Tweeti Çevir

ÖS 6:38 · 8 Ağu 2019 · Twitter Web App

Nick Szabo
@NickSzabo4

@NickSzabo4 @AStulkowski ve diğer 3 kişiye yanıt olarak

Obviously one cannot ship gold atoms as network data. And I saw the failure of IOUs again, now digital (e-gold). So I needed to discover general principles of trust-minimized money I could apply to cyberspace. For that I studied other forms of early (trust-minimized) money.

Tweeti Çevir

ÖS 7:14 · 8 Ağu 2019 · Twitter Web App

Nick Szabo
@NickSzabo4

@NickSzabo4 @AStulkowski ve diğer 3 kişiye yanıt olarak

From thinking about what monetary metals, shells, diamonds, rare postage stamps, ... had in common, and applying historically recent computer science breakthroughs to implement those principles in a trust-minimized way on a digital network, came bit gold: nakamotoinstitute.org/bit-gold/

Tweeti Çevir

ÖS 7:20 · 8 Ağu 2019 · Twitter Web App

Is Nick szabo Satoshi Nakamoto? May be. Who knows!

Scan the QR code to see the tweet thread of Nick Szabo

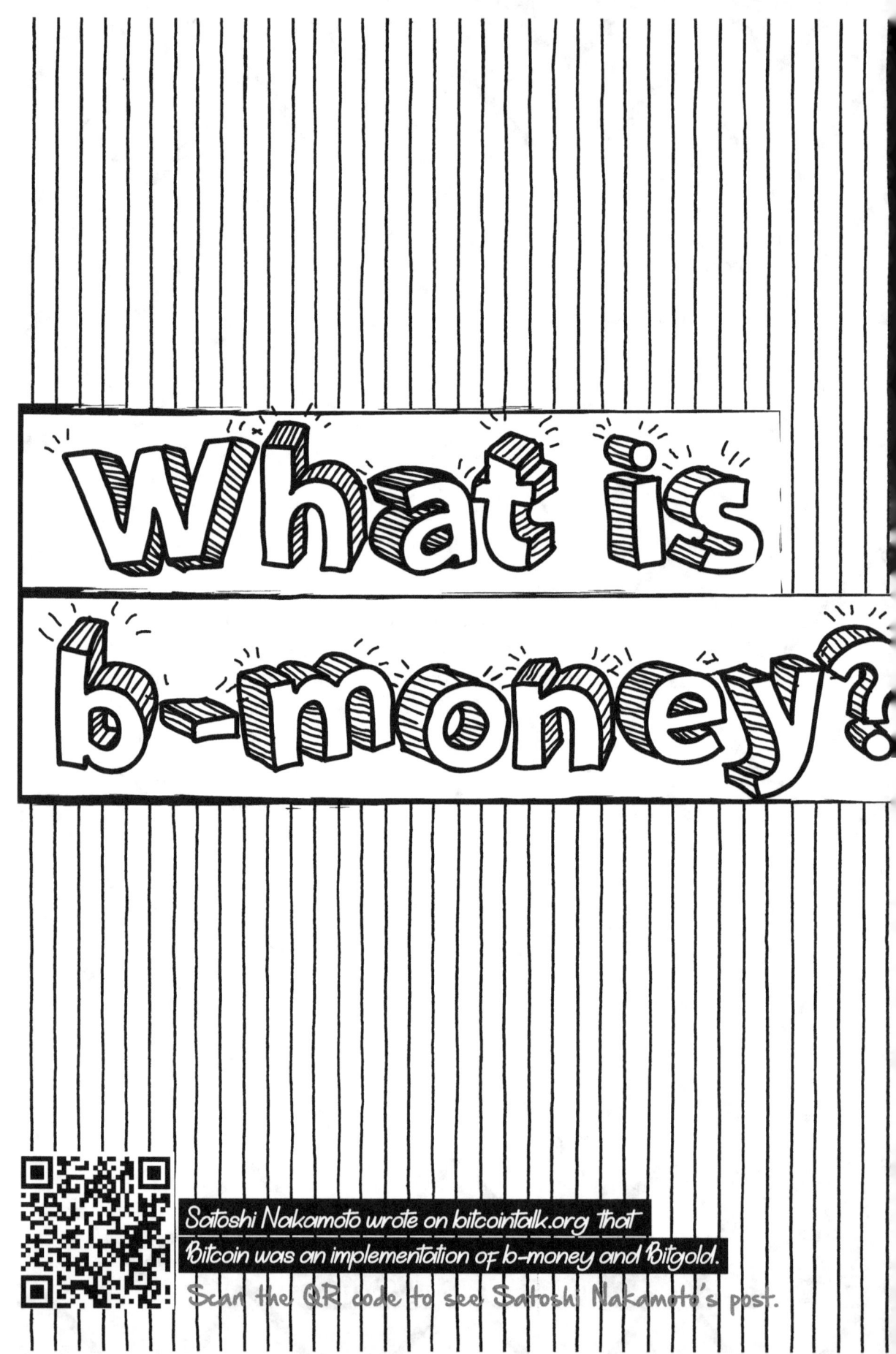

What is b-money?

Satoshi Nakamoto wrote on bitcointalk.org that Bitcoin was an implementation of b-money and Bitgold.

Scan the QR code to see Satoshi Nakamoto's post.

Scan the QR code
to see Wei Dai's b-money proposal

Moved by the "Crypto-Anarchist Manifest" of Tim May, Wei Dai believed that an anonymous and untraceable trading tool, namely a brand new currency and money transfer was required for a truly free and anonymous society to exist in the cyber realm. What Wei Dai suggested in this regard was "b-money" in 1998. B-money remained only on paper and was never realized.

What is RPOW?

(Reusable Proofs of Work)

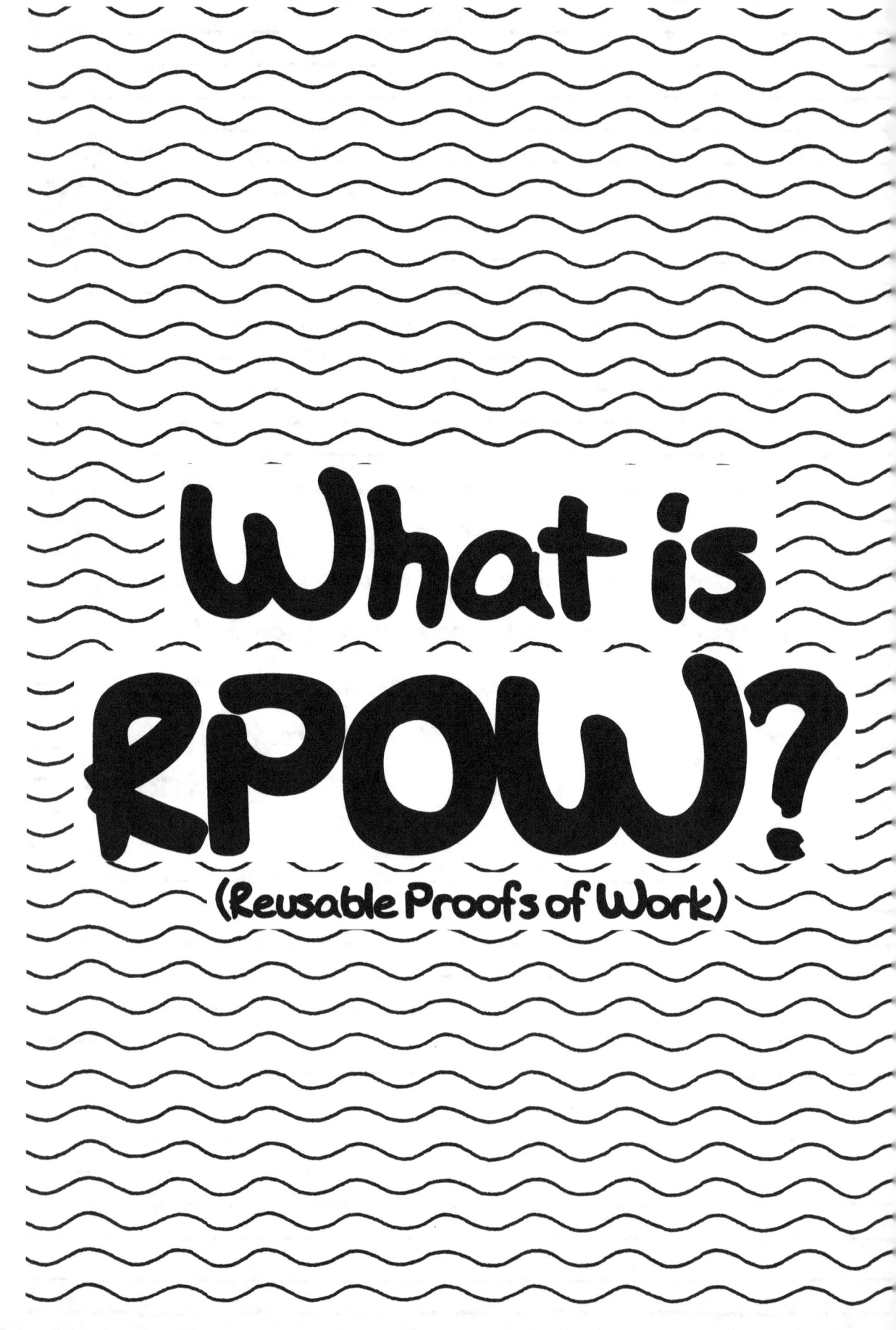

Inspired by Nick Szabo's "Collectibles" theory, Hal Finney developed RPOW. RPOW is based on the "Proof of Work" protocol, just like Bitcoin. From this perspective, RPOW may be considered as the first prototype of Bitcoin.

Contrary to Bitcoin, RPOW does have a trusted 3rd party (intermediary). A transparent "server" checks to see whether a double spending occurs and confirms the transaction when sending a "coin" from one person to another.

Acting as the trusted 3rd party, this "server" differs from the conventional "trusted 3rd parties" in that it has a transparent structure. But RPOW was not created for coming up with a monetary form.

Scan the QR code to see Hal Finney's RPOW proposal.

Was Milton Friedman talking about Bitcoin in 1999?

"Internet is going to be one of the major forces for reducing the role of government. The one thing that's missing but soon will be developed is a reliable e-cash"

Milton Friedman

Scan the QR Code
to watch the interview.

Bitcoin P2P e-cash paper 2008-11-01 19:16:33 UTC

I've been working on a new electronic cash system that's fully peer-to-peer, with no trusted third party.

The paper is available at:
http://www.bitcoin.org/bitcoin.pdf

The main properties:
Double-spending is prevented with a peer-to-peer network.
No mint or other trusted parties.
Participants can be anonymous.
New coins are made from Hashcash style proof-of-work.
The proof-of-work for new coin generation also powers the network to prevent double-spending.

Bitcoin: A Peer-to-Peer Electronic Cash Svstem

Abstract. A purely peer-to-peer version of electronic cash would allow online payments to be sent directly from one party to another without the burdens of going through a financial institution. Digital signatures provide part of the solution, but the main benefits are lost if a trusted party is still required to prevent double-spending. We propose a solution to the double-spending problem using a peer-to-peer network. The network timestamps transactions by hashing them into an ongoing chain of hash-based proof-of-work, forming a record that cannot be changed without redoing the proof-of-work. The longest chain not only serves as proof of the sequence of events witnessed, but proof that it came from the largest pool of CPU power. As long as honest nodes control the most CPU power on the network, they can generate the longest chain and outpace any attackers. The network itself requires minimal structure. Messages are broadcasted on a best effort basis, and nodes can leave and rejoin the network at will, accepting the longest proof-of-work chain as proof of what happened while they were gone.

Full paper at:
http://www.bitcoin.org/bitcoin.pdf

Satoshi Nakamoto

The Cryptography Mailing List
Unsubscribe by sending "unsubscribe cryptography" to

First e-mail containing the Bitcoin white paper shared by Satoshi Nakamoto in the Cryptography Mail Group

Mail announcing that the 1st version of Bitcoin software is ready, shared by Satoshi Nakamoto in the Cryptography Mail Group

Bitcoin v0.1 released 2009-01-09 20:05:49 UTC

```
Announcing the first release of Bitcoin, a new electronic cash
system that uses a peer-to-peer network to prevent double-spending.
It's completely decentralized with no server or central authority.

See bitcoin.org for screenshots.

Download link:
http://downloads.sourceforge.net/bitcoin/bitcoin-0.1.0.rar

Windows only for now. Open source C++ code is included.

- Unpack the files into a directory
- Run BITCOIN.EXE
- It automatically connects to other nodes

If you can keep a node running that accepts incoming connections,
you'll really be helping the network a lot. Port 8333 on your
firewall needs to be open to receive incoming connections.

The software is still alpha and experimental. There's no guarantee
the system's state won't have to be restarted at some point if it
becomes necessary, although I've done everything I can to build in
extensibility and versioning.

You can get coins by getting someone to send you some, or turn on
Options->Generate Coins to run a node and generate blocks. I made
the proof-of-work difficulty ridiculously easy to start with, so
for a little while in the beginning a typical PC will be able to
generate coins in just a few hours. It'll get a lot harder when
competition makes the automatic adjustment drive up the difficulty.
Generated coins must wait 120 blocks to mature before they can be
spent.

There are two ways to send money. If the recipient is online, you
can enter their IP address and it will connect, get a new public
key and send the transaction with comments. If the recipient is
not online, it is possible to send to their Bitcoin address, which
is a hash of their public key that they give you. They'll receive
the transaction the next time they connect and get the block it's
in. This method has the disadvantage that no comment information
is sent, and a bit of privacy may be lost if the address is used
multiple times, but it is a useful alternative if both users can't
be online at the same time or the recipient can't receive incoming
connections.

Total circulation will be 21,000,000 coins. It'll be distributed
to network nodes when they make blocks, with the amount cut in half
every 4 years.

first 4 years: 10,500,000 coins
next 4 years: 5,250,000 coins
next 4 years: 2,625,000 coins
next 4 years: 1,312,500 coins
etc...

When that runs out, the system can support transaction fees if
needed. It's based on open market competition, and there will
probably always be nodes willing to process transactions for free.

Satoshi Nakamoto

---------------------------------------------------------------------
The Cryptography Mailing List
Unsubscribe by sending "unsubscribe cryptography" to
majord...@metzdowd.com
```

why other
untraceable
electronic
money transfer
systems
cannot be
successful?

When Satoshi Nakamoto published the first version of Bitcoin, it was mentioned that there was an initiative called "Open Coin" in the UK, to which he replied:

"A lot of people automtically dismiss e-currency as a lost beacuse of all the companies that failed since the 1990's. I hope it's obvious it was only the centrally controlled nature of those systems that doomed them.

I think this is the first time we're trying a decentralized, non-trust-based system."

Why do we need trusted 3rd parties?

The trading system has gradually grown and became increasingly complicated throughout the centuries. Everyone became able to trade with anyone on a global scale. In order to keep the relevant information safe, these transactions were first recorded in ledgers, then in computers. As time progressed and technology advanced, the methods we use for keeping these transactions have changed, but the mostly non-public and isolated manner of managing the information remained the same. That is why we always needed an intermediary person, institution to verify or have others verify, approve said information so far. These intermediaries have always been called the "trusted third parties" on the assumption that they are indeed trustworthy.

Who is the most trusted 3rd party?

God

Imagine the ideal protocol. It would have the most trustworthy third party imaginable – a diety who is on everybody's side.

Alas, in the our temporal world we deal with humans rather than deities. Yet, too often we are forced to treat people in a nearly theological manner, because our infrastructure lacks the security needed to protect ourselves.

Nick Szabo, The God Protocols

To read "The God Protocols" paper by Nick Szabo scan the QR code.

Don't
trust
verify

When Satoshi Nakamoto was creating Bitcoin, he was proposing an alternative to all transactions occurring between two parties that required a trusted 3rd party:

"Let's stop trusting a 3rd party we deem to be trustworthy in transactions occurring between two people. Instead, let's look at the encrypted proofs."

To put it simply, Satoshi Nakamoto was proposing **a rational mindset instead of an unquestioned trust/faith in all trusted 3rd parties... people, banks, corporations, states.**

what is the main difference between existing centralized financial system and bitcoin's decentralized structure?

CENTRALIZED SYSTEMS

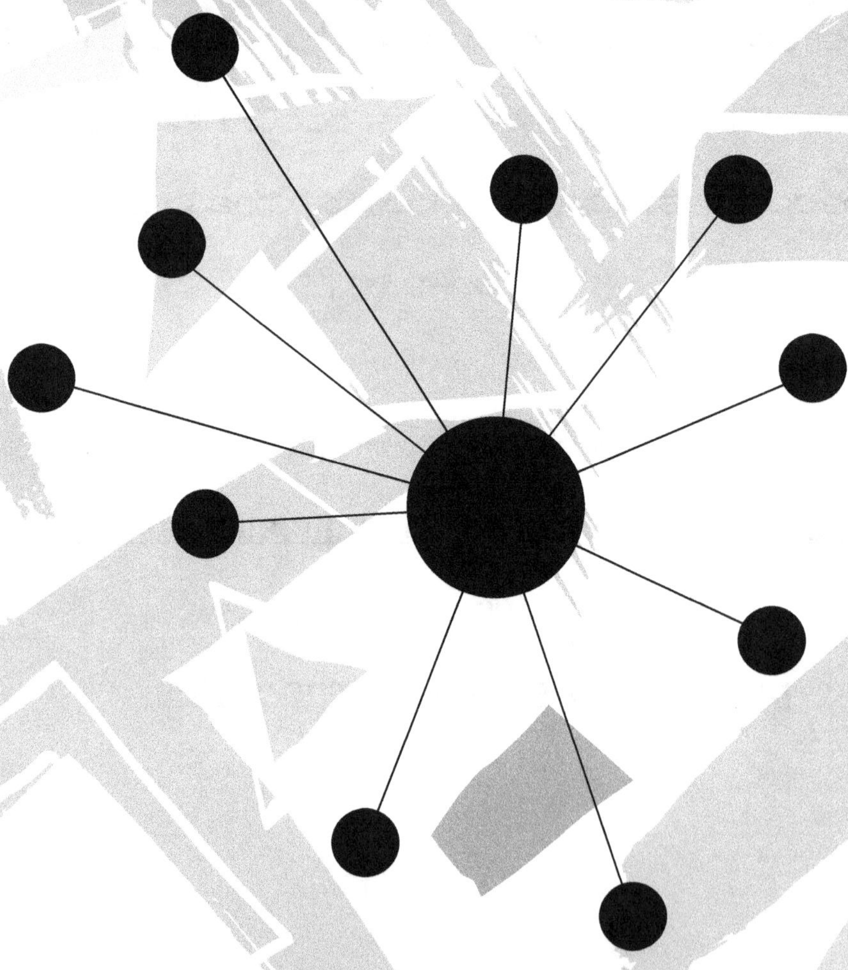

DECENTRALIZED SYSTEMS

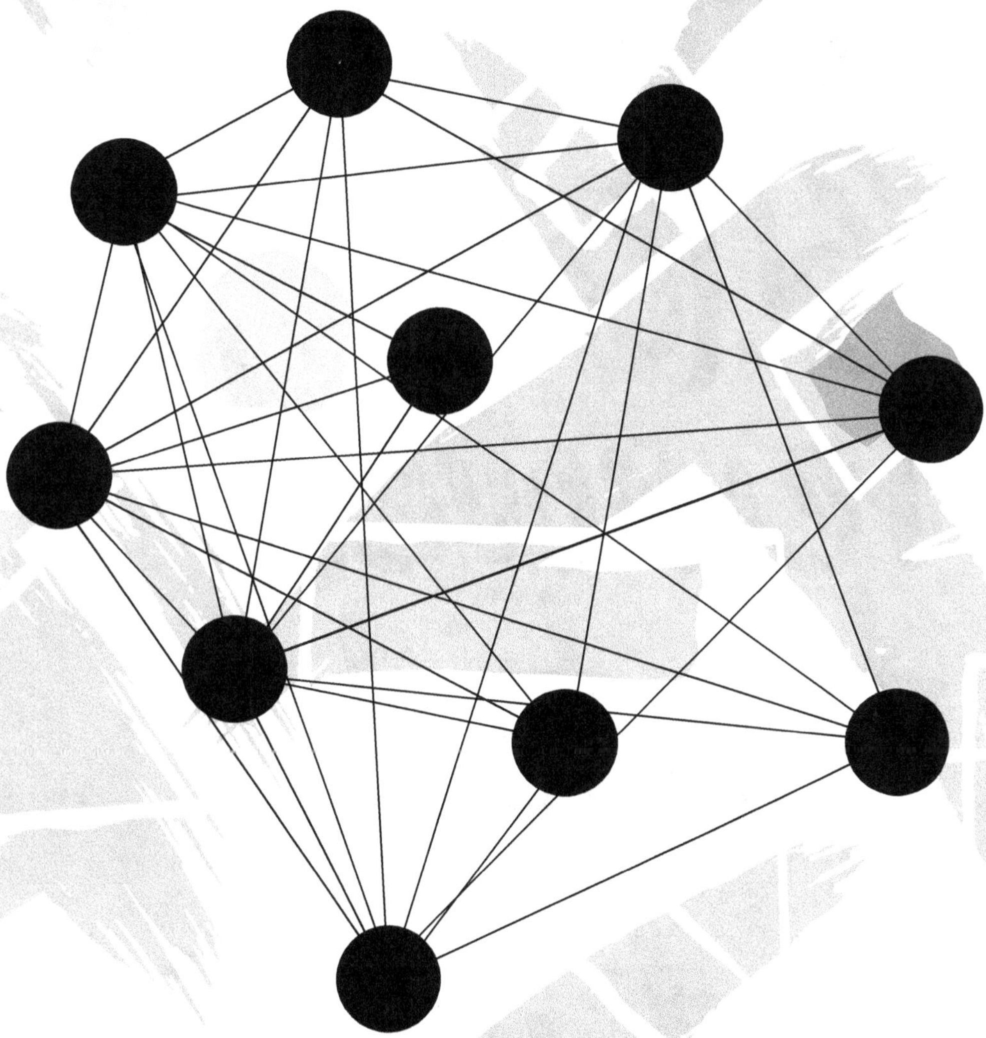

Contrary to existing centralized systems Bitcoin's decentralized structure doesn't have a single point of failure.

How Bitcoin removed trusted 3rd parties?

Bitcoin blockchain enables a computer network which has all of its components connected to the Internet and which can record and keep all of the performed transfers and transactions, to store the whole process in the computers distributed across said network. Also, joining the network is completely free of charge and the system is open to anyone who wants partake in the process with their computers. The execution of the process in this manner prevents the transactions from being in a closed circuit or from being managed by a single person/ institution. Instead,

the information is recorded on and accessible from a single digital ledger which distributed throughout the whole network.

Bitcoin is not really a "virtual currency"; it is simply an application that runs on the basis of the blockchain software and is supported by cryptography due to its working principles.

Want
to learn
Bitcoin
from
its
creator?

Bitcoin: A Peer-to-Peer Electronic Cash System

A purely peer-to-peer version of electronic cash would allow online payments to be sent directly from one party to another without going through a financial institution. Digital signatures provide part of the solution, but the main benefits are lost if a trusted third party is still required to prevent double-spending. We propose a solution to the double-spending problem using a peer-to-peer network. The network timestamps transactions by hashing them into an ongoing chain of hash-based proof-of-work, forming a record that cannot be changed without redoing the proof-ofwork. The longest chain not only serves as proof of the sequence of events witnessed, but proof that it came from the largest pool of CPU power. As long as a majority of CPU power is controlled by nodes that are not cooperating to attack the network, they will generate the longest chain and outpace attackers. The network itself requires minimal structure. Messages are broadcast on a best effort basis, and nodes can leave and rejoin the network at will, accepting the longest proof-of-work chain as proof of what happened while they were gone.

Scan the QR code
to read the
"Bitcoin Whitepaper".

Satoshi Nakamoto

THE NATURE OF BITCOIN IS SUCH THAT ONCE VERSION 0.1 WAS RELEASED,

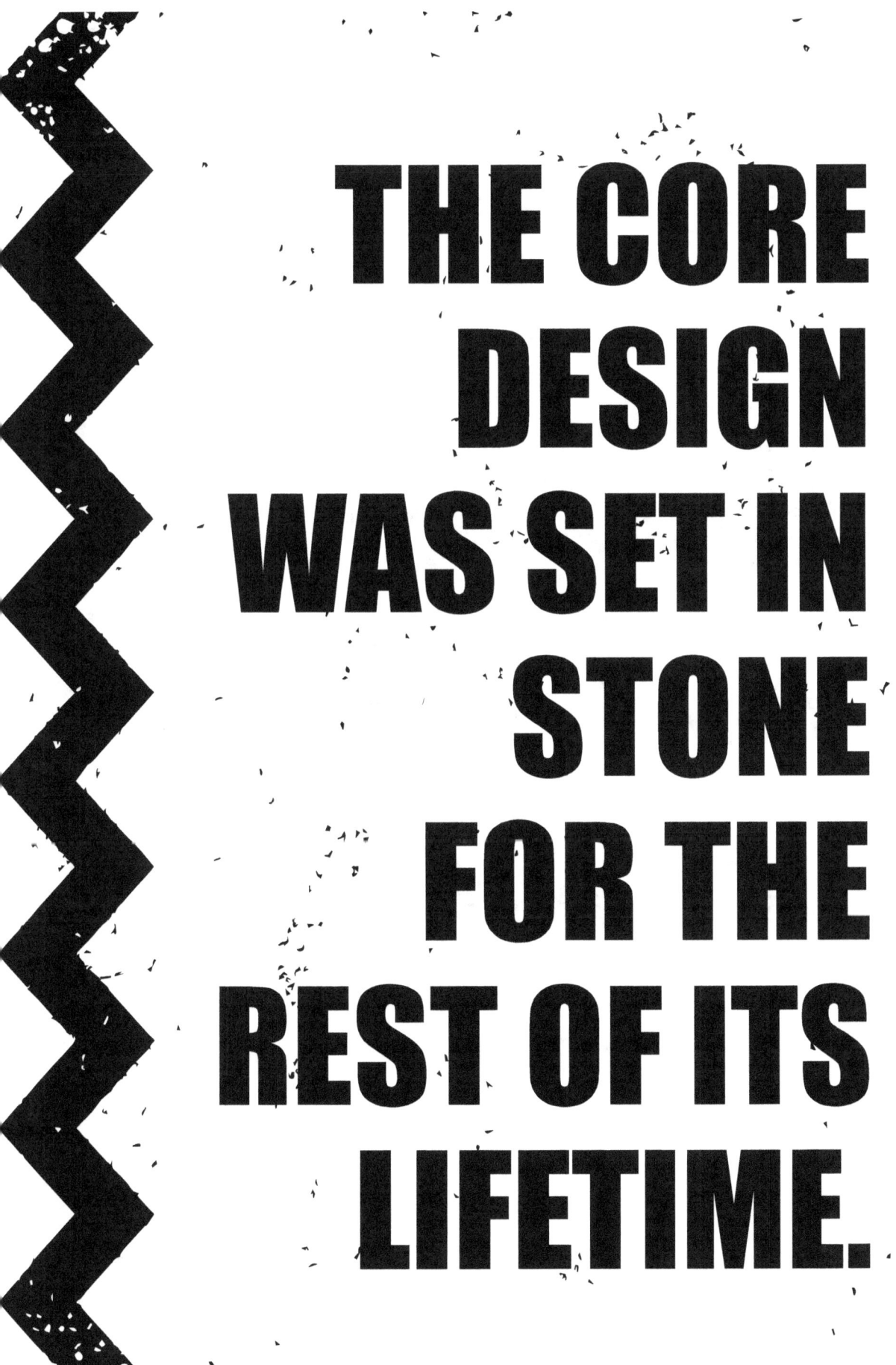

THE CORE DESIGN WAS SET IN STONE FOR THE REST OF ITS LIFETIME.

How are new bitcoins created?

By Mining

WHAT IS BITCOIN MINING?

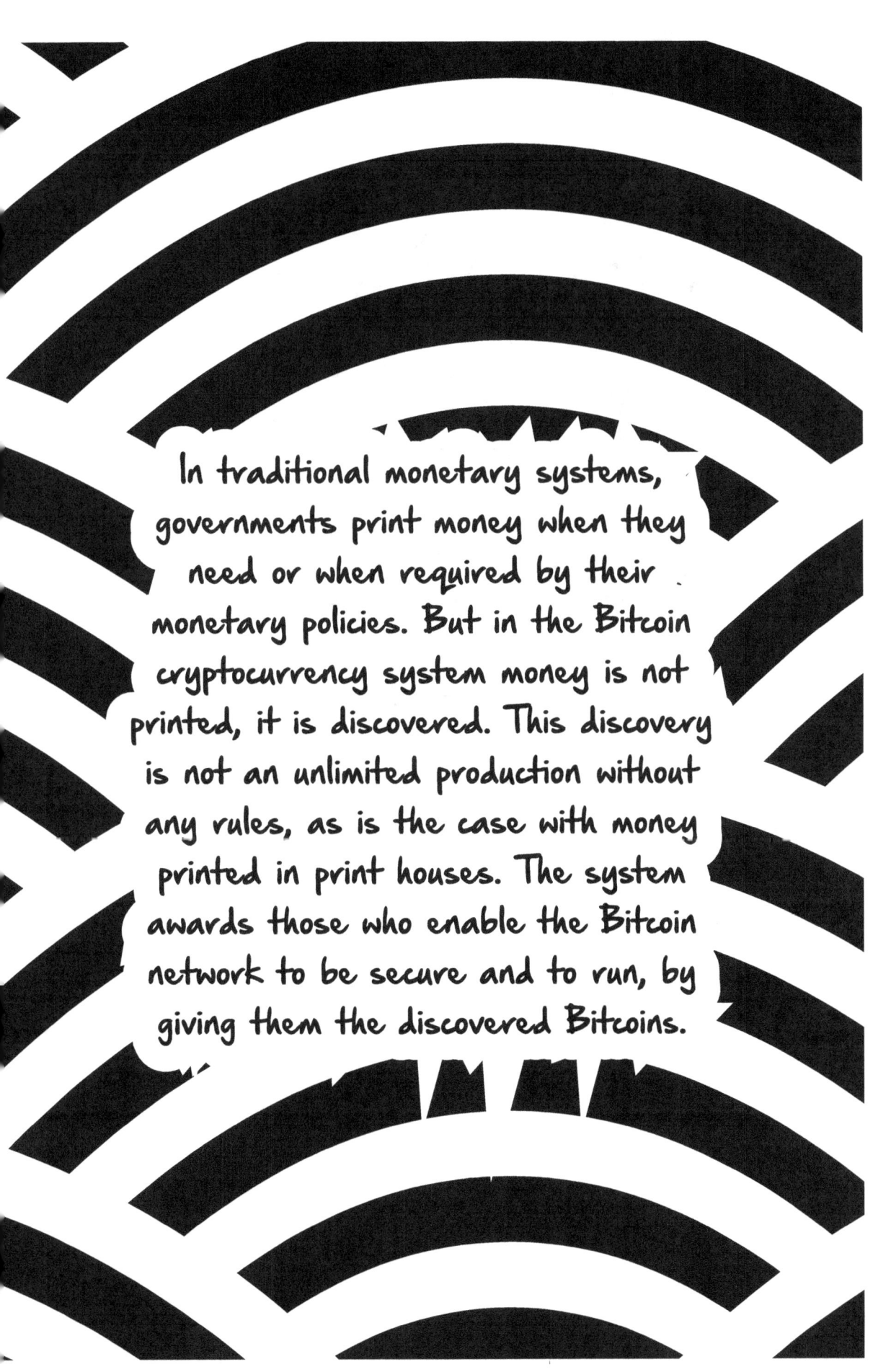

In traditional monetary systems, governments print money when they need or when required by their monetary policies. But in the Bitcoin cryptocurrency system money is not printed, it is discovered. This discovery is not an unlimited production without any rules, as is the case with money printed in print houses. The system awards those who enable the Bitcoin network to be secure and to run, by giving them the discovered Bitcoins.

DO WE KNOW MINING SCHEDULE OF BITCOIN?

2009–2012......Block reward = 50 BTC

2012–2016......Block reward = 25 BTC

2016–2020......Block reward = 12,5 BTC

2020–2024.....Block reward = 6,25 BTC

....

....

....

....

21.000.000 bitcoins will be available around the year 2141.
Bitcoin block reward is halved every four years.

How about your national fiat currency issuing schedule?
Oh sorry, it is based on politics, you never know!

Who is the first person started mining after Satoshi Nakamoto?

First block –Genesis Block– was mined
on January 3, 2009 by Satoshi Nakamoto.
Hal Finney tweeted that he was running Bitcoin
on 10 January, 2009.
This tweet also is the first tweet about Bitcoin.
Is Hal Finney Satoshi Nakamoto?
Who knows?

halfin
@halfin
Follow
Running bitcoin
7:33 PM - 10 Jan 2009
1,843 Retweets 4,408 Likes
164
1.8K
4.4K

How can you store your Bitcoins?

Fundamentally, bitcoin wallets exist for three reasons.

1. Seeing the current bitcoin balance
2. Buying and sending bitcoins
3. Storing and keeping bitcoins

To reinforce with an easy example, wallets are not that different from the interfaces and applications you use for sending/receiving e-mails in principle. Just as we need such interfaces to send or receive our e-mails, we need Bitcoin wallets for basically the same reason.

Scan the QR code
to learn about Bitcoin wallets.

Traditional currencies have no limit of supply!

IS THERE A SUPPLY LIMIT OF BITCOIN?

Unlike fiat currencies there is a limited supply of Bitcoin. It's monetary policy has been determined in advance.

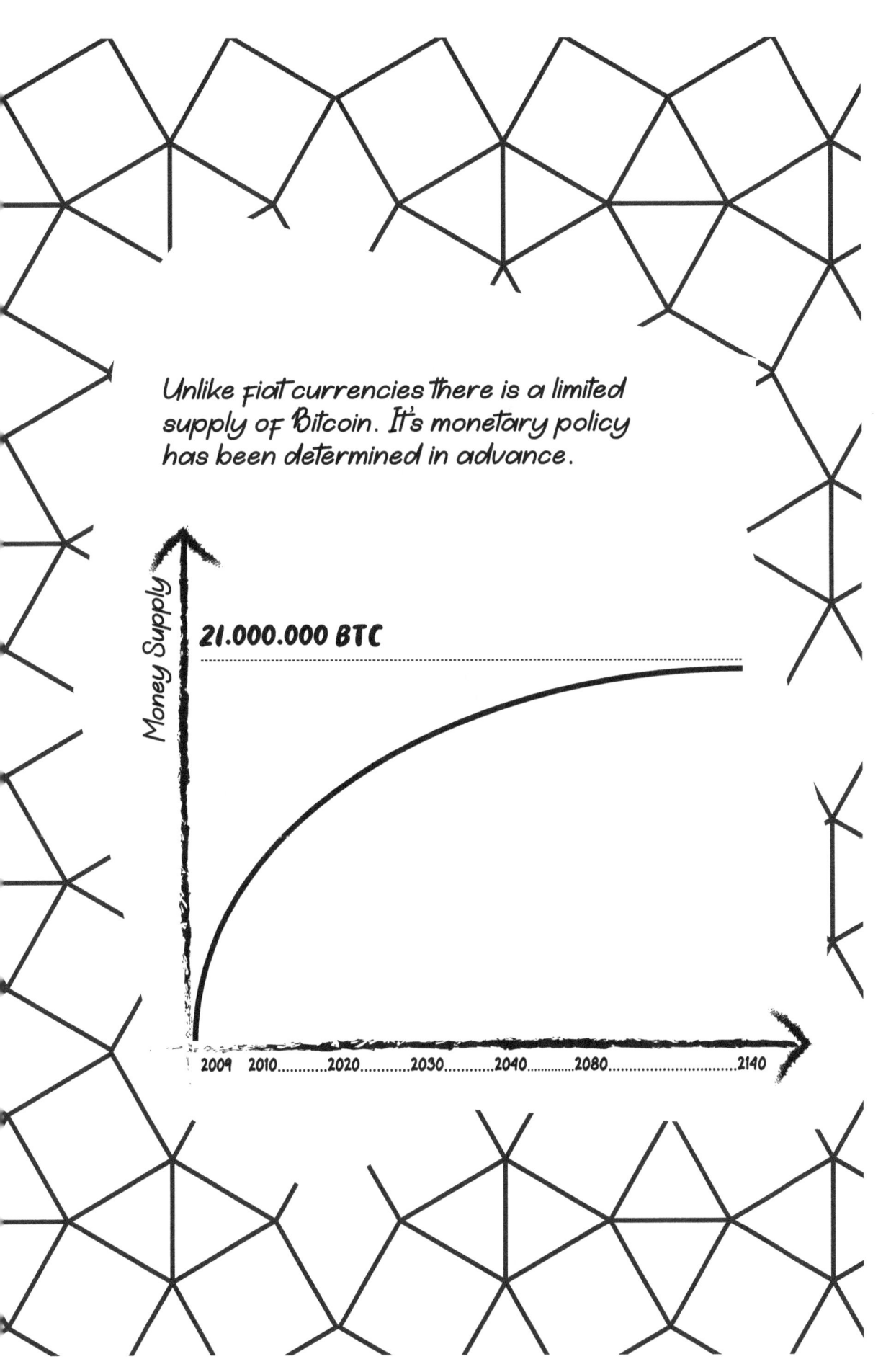

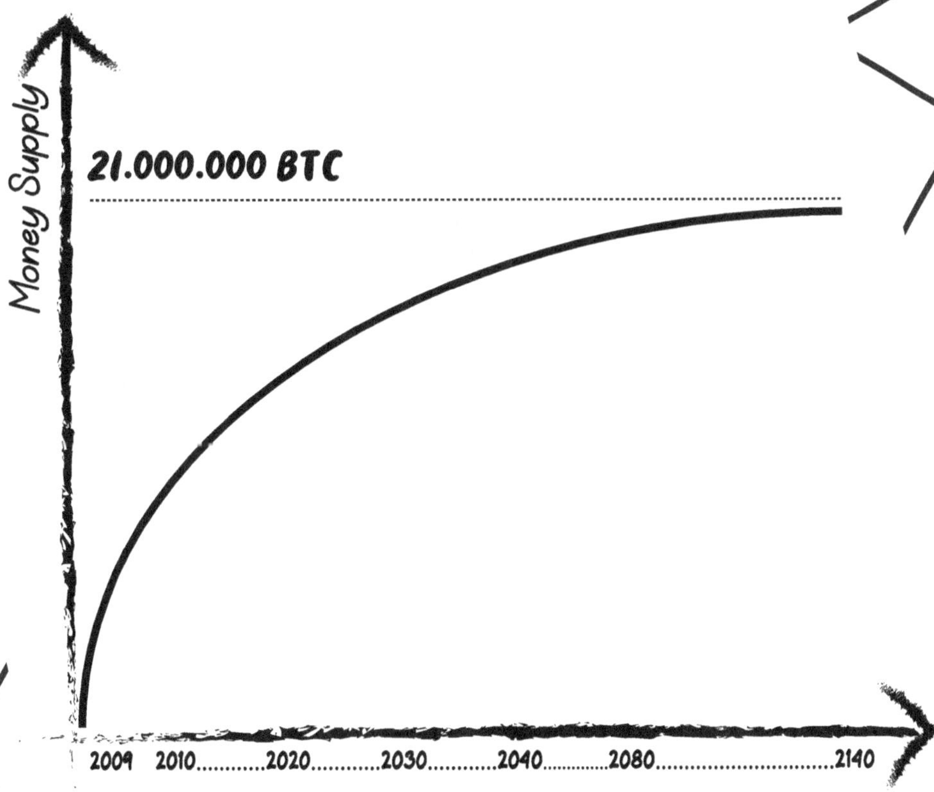

What does 1 BTC = 1 BTC mean?

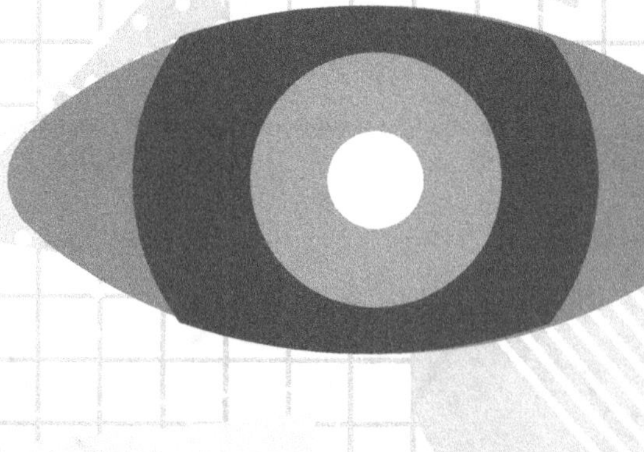

The only price chart that matters

It means that
1 BTC is always 1/21.000.000 of the total reserve.
It's based on mathematics not politics.

In traditional currencies issuing money is based on politics. And purchasing power of your money is eroded by politicians.

What was the first public sale price of Bitcoin?

1 USD = 1309 BTC

October 5, 2009

How was it calculated?

A stock exchange called New Liberty Standard allowed BTC to be bought via PayPal.

Here is how they calculated the exchange rate:

Our exchange rate is calculated by dividing $1.00 by the average amount of electricity required to run a computer with high CPU for a year, 1331.5 kWh, multiplied by the the average residential cost of electricity in the United States for the previous year, $0.1136, divided by 12 months divided by the number of bitcoins generated by my computer over the past 30 days.

Scan the QR code to see the exchange rates of New Liberty Standard in 2009

Who designed the Bitcoin logo?

Final version of Bitcoin logo is designed by a bitcointalk.org user whose nickname is “bitboy”.

WHAT IS *the unofficial mascot* OF BITCOIN?

Why do you think?

Scan the QR code
to learn more about honey badgers.

What is the name of the smallest unit of bitcoin?

Smallest unit of bitcoin is called Satoshi after its creator.

1 SATOSHI

=

1/100.000.000 BTC

or 0,00000001 BTC

Who made the first Bitcoin transaction?

Satoshi Nakamoto sent 10 BTC
to Hal Finney on 12 January 2009.
It was a transaction for test.
But Hal Finney forgot to sent it back.

(At the time Hal Finney was
helping to Bitcoin creator Satoshi Nakamoto with the code.)

Scan the QR Code
to see this transaction on Bitcoin blockchain.

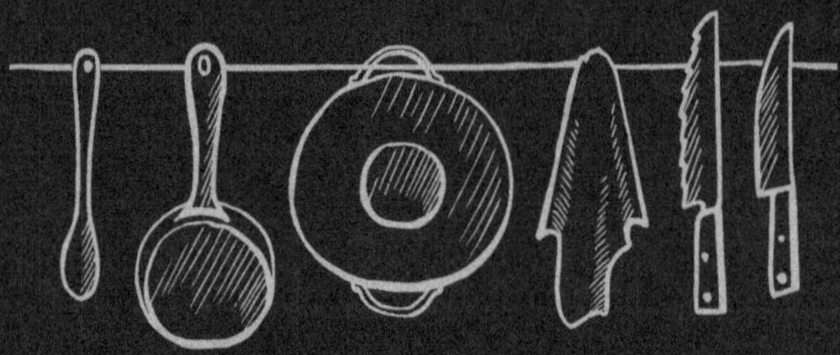

Why do people celebrate BITCOIN PIZZA DAY?

Laszlo Hanyecz bought two pizzas with Bitcoin on 22 May 2010. It is recognized as the first real-world transaction with Bitcoin. Laszlo paid 10.000 Bitcoin to another Bitcoin Forum user who ordered two Papa John's pizzas for Laszlo.

Most expensive pizza of the world:
Two pizzas now costs approximately 12.000.000 USD
-July 2019-

Visit:
To see the whole story on Bitcoin forum scan the QRcode.

HOW MANY TIMES DID BITCOIN DIE?

According to trusted media
Bitcoin died 373 times
until now. (September 1, 2019 :)

Scan the QR
to see the current
number :)

IS BITCOIN USED FOR ILLEGAL ACTIVITIES?

Bitcoin was invented in 2009.
Weren't drugs being sold
in the world before 2009?
Or, how much of the global drug trade
is done via Bitcoin?
Weren't terror funds transferred via
the existing banking system before?
Isn't the dollar still being used
in these illegal activities?

Which headline from The Times is included in the code of the Bitcoin Genesis Block?

For, you can see the headline of The Times dated Jan 3, 2009 in the code contained in the Genesis block of Bitcoin: "The Times 03/Jan 2009. Chancellor on brink of second bailout for banks."

The content of the news article tells that the state considers the options of re-injecting the huge sums of money obtained from taxes back into the economy or taking on the toxic assets of banks. (Toxic assets are the assets that have almost no financial value.)

Scan the QR Code to see "the headline" in the Genesis Block.

THE TIMES

DIEU ET MON DROIT

Saturday January 3 2009 timesonline.co.uk

£1.50

Eat Out from £5

More than 900 great restaurants, including four **Gordon Ramsay** favourites from £15

Start collecting tokens today Pullout inside

Israel prepares to send tanks and troops into Gaza

Israel allowed foreigners to flee the Gaza Strip as it prepared for a ground offensive. At least 430 Palestinians were killed in a week of airstrikes

Michael Sheen
Frost, Nixon and me

Working mums
So that's how she does it

Detox in style
The best spas on the planet

Travel

Salman Rushdie
I won't marry again

Giant killing?
Guide to the FA Cup third round

Sport

Chancellor on brink of second bailout for banks

Billions may be needed as lending squeeze tightens

Francis Elliott
Gary Duncan

99p

Pub chain cuts the price of a pint from £1.62 to 1989 levels
Business, page 47

Was Economist cover of January 1988 foretelling Bitcoin?

The cover of the Economist from January 1988 shows a gold-like coin on a chain around the neck of a phoenix rising from the ashes of burning dollars. The date on the coin is 2018. The tagline on the cover is: "Get ready for a world currency". Many thinks that Economist was foretelling the Bitcoin. Makes so much sense, right? No, it does not.

Actually, the story advocates that a single global currency would be better for "monetary policies" and "inflation." It says that a mismanaged monetary policy in one country would hurt not only her own economy, but also the economy of others in a world without walls or borders.

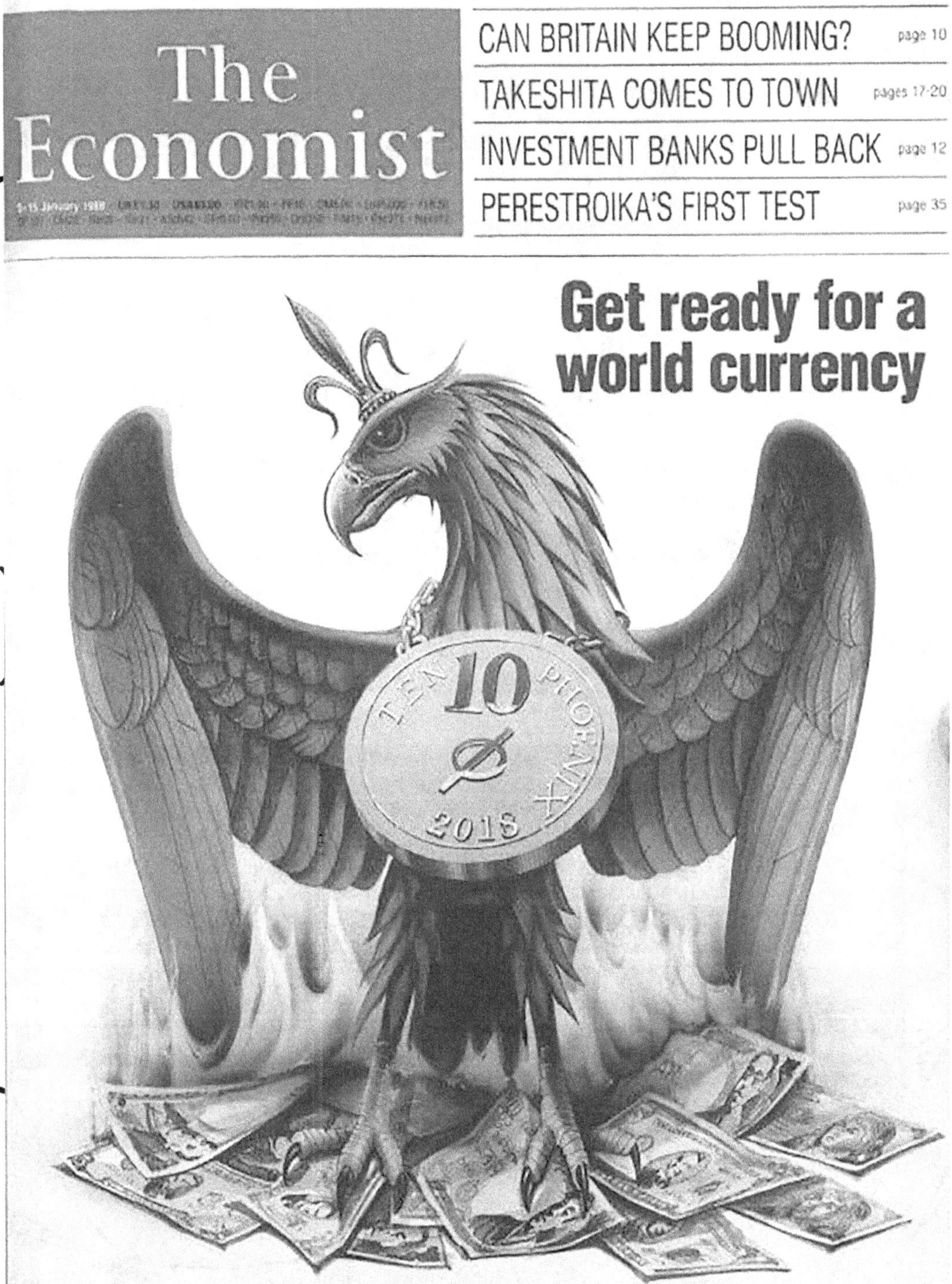
The Economist
CAN BRITAIN KEEP BOOMING? page 10
TAKESHITA COMES TO TOWN pages 17-20
INVESTMENT BANKS PULL BACK page 12
PERESTROIKA'S FIRST TEST page 35
Get ready for a world currency
TEN 10 PHOENIX
2018

Why is Satoshi Nakamoto a mystery?

Humanity used the bounty of the nature as money since day one. It means that, humans trusted a free currency that wasn't tied to anyone. In order for the revolution to succeed, Bitcoin needed to be transformed into an asset that was gifted to humanity by nature. For this reason, it was crucial that the creator(s) remained a mystery. Because you cannot separate any invention from its creator.

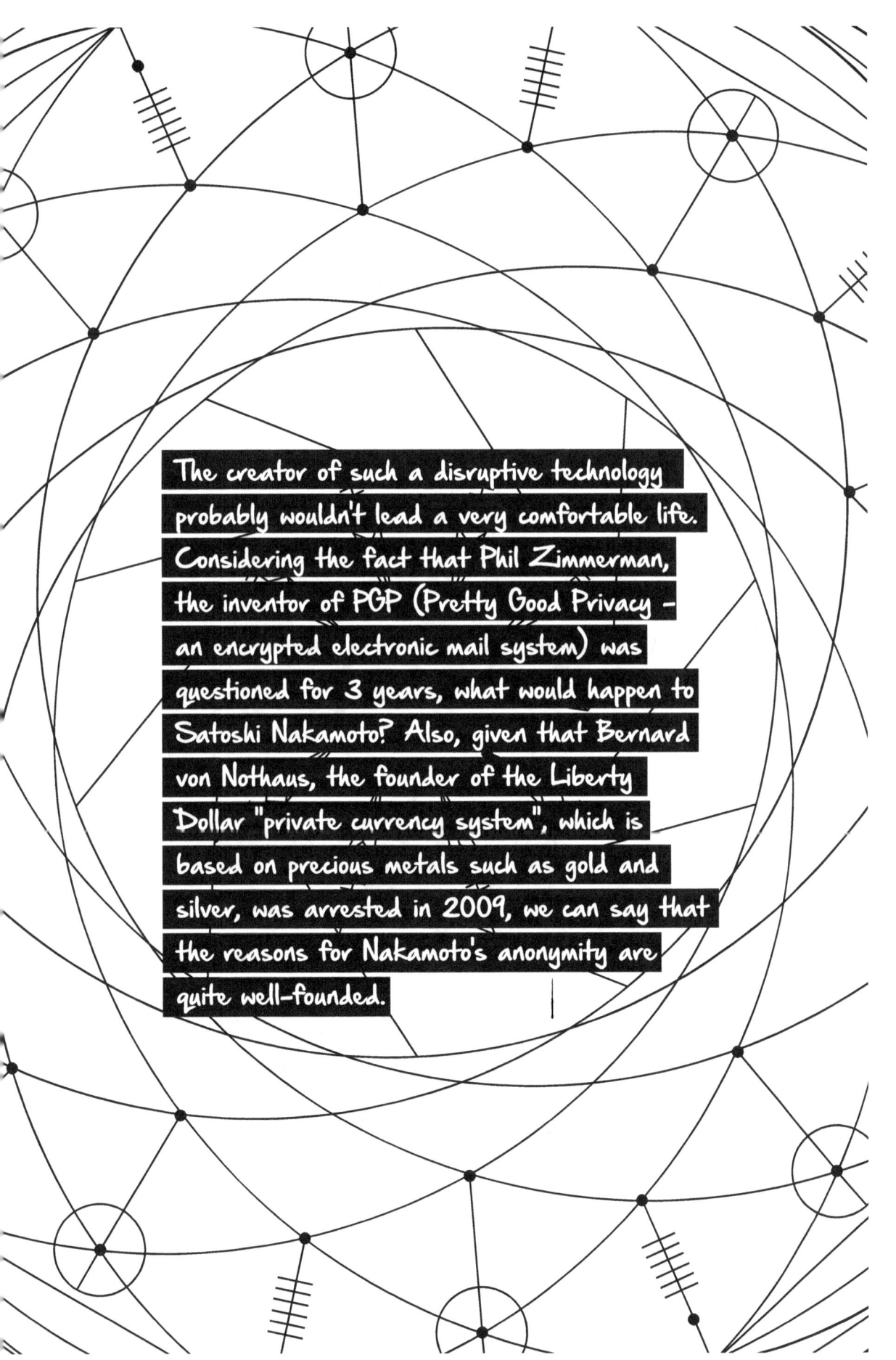

The creator of such a disruptive technology probably wouldn't lead a very comfortable life. Considering the fact that Phil Zimmerman, the inventor of PGP (Pretty Good Privacy – an encrypted electronic mail system) was questioned for 3 years, what would happen to Satoshi Nakamoto? Also, given that Bernard von Nothaus, the founder of the Liberty Dollar "private currency system", which is based on precious metals such as gold and silver, was arrested in 2009, we can say that the reasons for Nakamoto's anonymity are quite well-founded.

WHO IS SATOSHI NAKA-MOTO?

We don't know who is Satoshi Nakamoto.
But at least we do know who is not:)
Not Craig Wright!

What does Satoshi Nakamoto mean?

There is likely an allusion in the pseudonym chosen by the creator of Bitcoin; because it is a manifest by nature, it is attempting to create an alternative future and it already contains a jab at the deviance of the existing financial system in its Genesis block.

Looking at the match-ups of the Japanese words Satoshi and Nakamoto, the meaning that is closest to the spirit of Bitcoin is this:

"PHOENIX RISING FROM THE ASHES OF CENTRALIZATION"

APRIL 5, 1975

What does birth date of Satoshi Nakamoto imply?

On **April 5**, 1933 gold ownership is forbidden in USA.It was re-legalized again in **1975**.

POSTMASTER: PLEASE POST IN A CONSPICUOUS PLACE.—JAMES A. FARLEY, Postmaster General

UNDER EXECUTIVE ORDER OF THE PRESIDENT

Issued April 5, 1933

APRIL 5, 1933

all persons are required to deliver

ON OR BEFORE MAY 1, 1933

all GOLD COIN, GOLD BULLION, AND GOLD CERTIFICATES now owned by them to a Federal Reserve Bank, branch or agency, or to any member bank of the Federal Reserve System.

Executive Order

FORBIDDING THE HOARDING OF GOLD COIN, GOLD BULLION AND GOLD CERTIFICATES

[illegible]

FRANKLIN D. ROOSEVELT

THE WHITE HOUSE
April 5, 1933.

For Further Information Consult Your Local Bank

GOLD CERTIFICATES may be identified by the words "GOLD CERTIFICATE" appearing thereon. The serial number and the Treasury seal on the face of a GOLD CERTIFICATE are printed in YELLOW. Be careful not to confuse GOLD CERTIFICATES with other issues which are redeemable in gold but which are not GOLD CERTIFICATES. Federal Reserve Notes and United States Notes are "redeemable in gold" but are not "GOLD CERTIFICATES" and are not required to be surrendered

Special attention is directed to the exceptions allowed under Section 2 of the Executive Order

CRIMINAL PENALTIES FOR VIOLATION OF EXECUTIVE ORDER
$10,000 fine or 10 years imprisonment, or both, as provided in Section 9 of the order

[illegible]
Secretary of the Treasury.

U.S. Government Printing Office: 1933 2-16064

Is bitcoin better than gold?

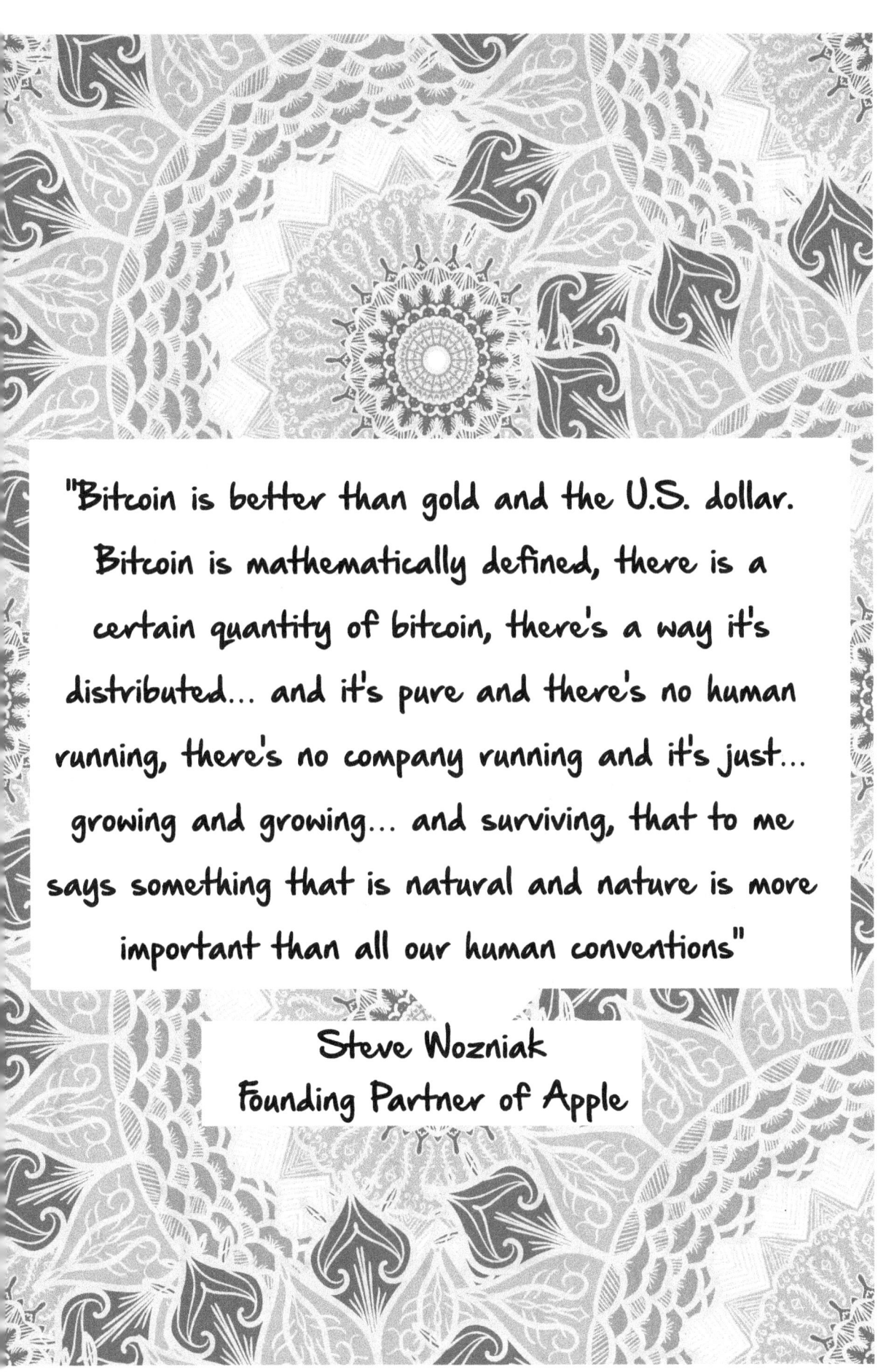

"Bitcoin is better than gold and the U.S. dollar. Bitcoin is mathematically defined, there is a certain quantity of bitcoin, there's a way it's distributed... and it's pure and there's no human running, there's no company running and it's just... growing and growing... and surviving, that to me says something that is natural and nature is more important than all our human conventions"

Steve Wozniak
Founding Partner of Apple

Is Bitcoin store of value or medium of exchange?

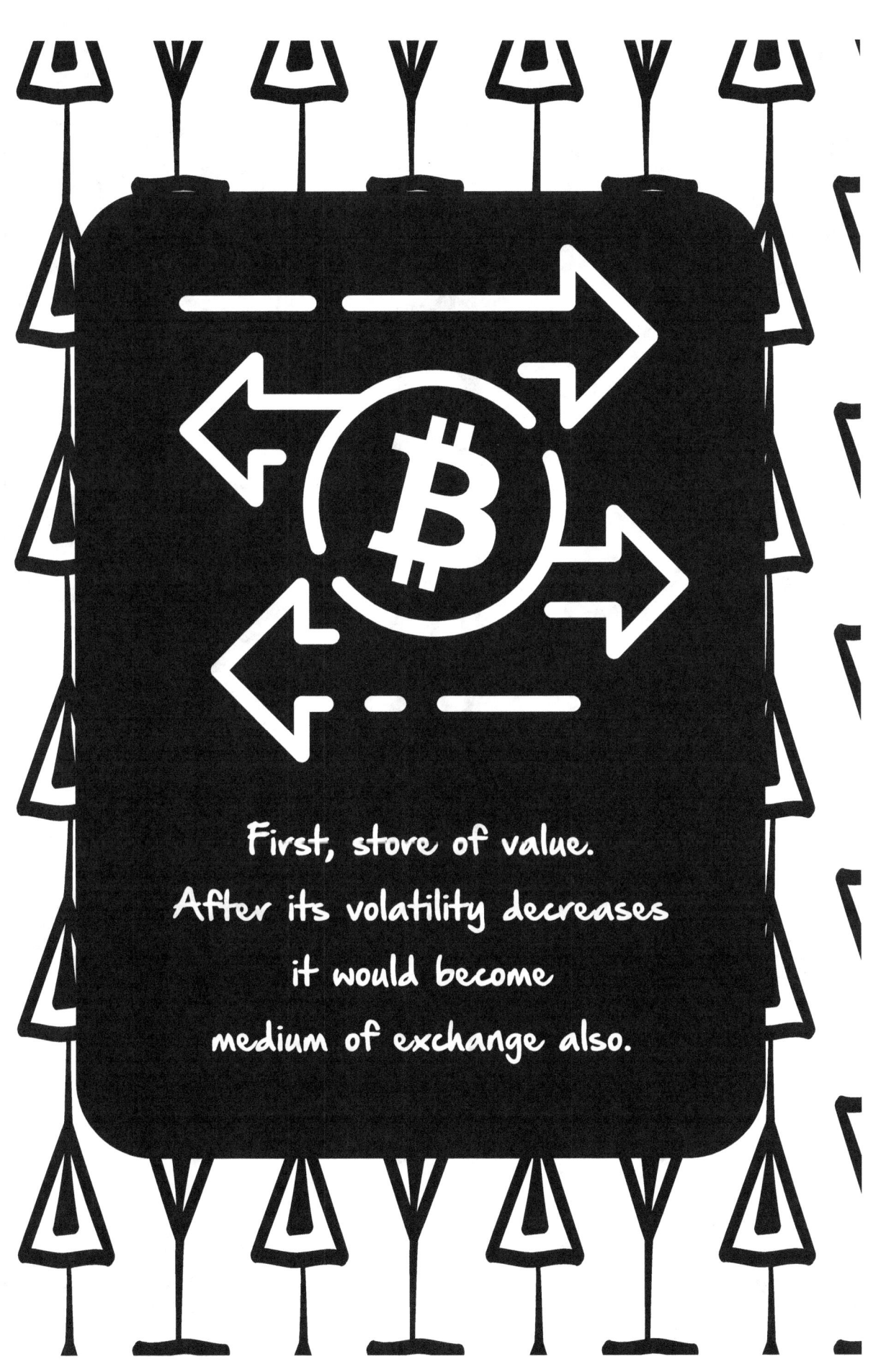

First, store of value.
After its volatility decreases
it would become
medium of exchange also.

RECOMMENDED BOOKS?

1) Bitcoin Standard
The Decentralized Alternative to Central Banking

Saifedean Ammous

2) Bitcoin:
Ayn Rand was Wrong. Atlas Never Shrugged!

Tuna Özen & Saadettin Konukseven

3) Programming Bitcoin:
Learn How to Program Bitcoin from Scratch

Jimmy Song

4) Inventing Bitcoin:
The Technology Behind the First Truly Scarce and Decentralized Money Explained

Yan Pritzker

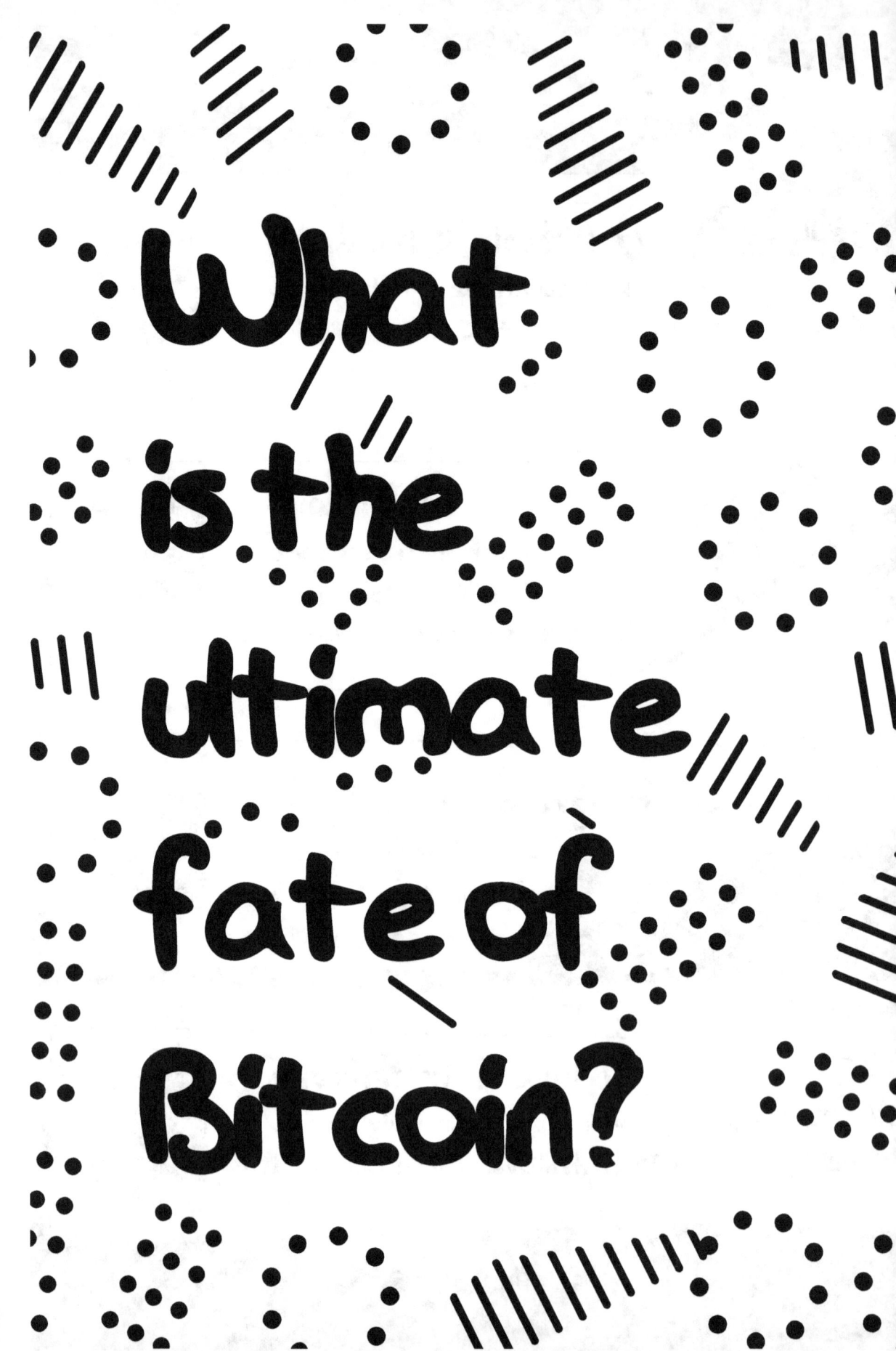

What is the ultimate fate of Bitcoin?

When Hal Finney made this comment, Bitcoin was 0,3 USD. Yes, just 30 cents!

I BELIEVE THIS WILL BE THE ULTIMATE FATE OF BITCOIN, TO BE THE

"HIGH-POWERED MONEY" THAT SERVES AS A RESERVE CURRENCY FOR BANKS

THAT ISSUE THEIR OWN DIGITAL CASH. MOST BITCOIN TRANSACTIONS WILL OCCUR BETWEEN BANKS, TO SETTLE NET TRANSFERS. BITCOIN TRANSACTIONS BY PRIVATE INDIVIDUALS WILL BE AS RARE AS WELL AS BITCOIN BASED PURCHASES ARE TODAY.

HAL FINNEY, 30.12.2010

Scan the QR code to read the full post of Hal Finney on bitcointalk.org.

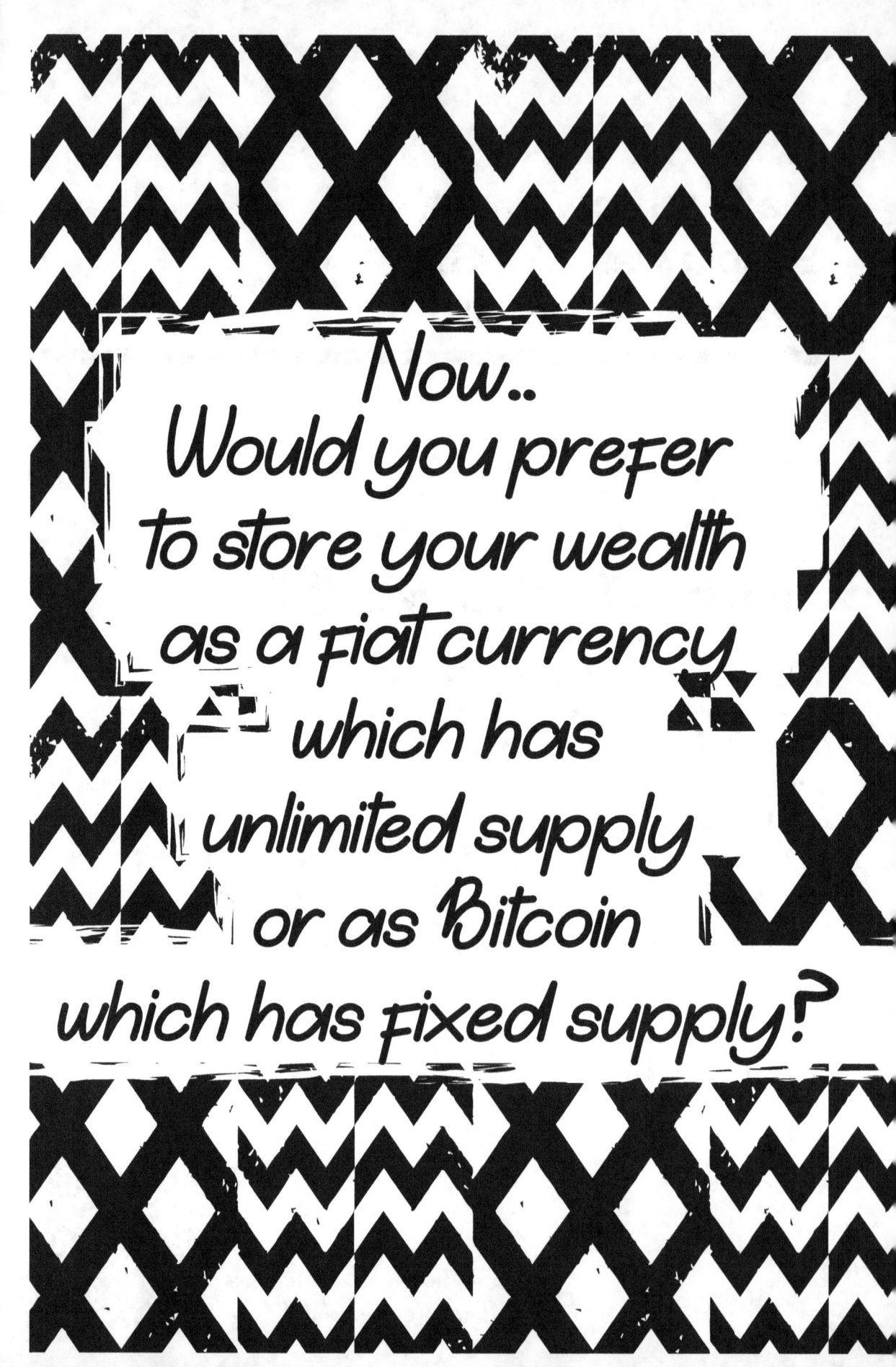

Now..
Would you prefer
to store your wealth
as a fiat currency
which has
unlimited supply
or as Bitcoin
which has fixed supply?

Write down your answer:

faqthebitcoin.com